HOW TO PUNCH THE SUNDAY JITTERS IN
THE FACE

*The High Performance Blueprint for
Unstoppable CEOs & Founders*

HOW TO PUNCH THE SUNDAY JITTERS IN
THE FACE

*The High Performance Blueprint for
Unstoppable CEOs & Founders*

TK KADER

Interior layout and design by Writing Nights.
Book preparation by Chad Robertson.
Cover Design by Ivica Jandrijevic.

For information about permission to reproduce selections from this book, email hello@getunstoppable.com.

Or write:

TK Kader
3111 N. Houston Street, PH1
Dallas, Texas 75219

ISBN: 979-8-3525-2284-4

Printed on acid free paper in the United States of America.

24   23   22   21   20   19   18   17   8   7   6   5   4   3   2   1

Here's to *you*. May you become *Unstoppable*.

PREFACE

They say everyone has a book inside of them. Here's the context on why I first wrote this book back in 2019, what happened after, and why I decided to publish a revamped 2nd edition now.

Back in 2019, I had just closed out my journey as a Venture-Backed CEO after exiting my SaaS business, then serving as SVP of Strategy at the SaaS company that bought mine and helping them sell it to Adobe. I asked myself: What's next? I was only 36 and I felt like I was just getting started.

Here was the problem: What they don't tell you when you sell your company is that you also sell the purpose that brought you daily fulfillment. I learned very quickly that true fulfillment is perhaps the most expensive thing in the world that even money cannot buy. Everyone has their own definition of fulfillment. For me – it was that thing you woke up every morning for, that thing you made your bed for, that thing you felt when you looked at yourself in the mirror as you brushed your teeth and said "Let's go get it." That thing. That's fulfillment (to me). And yet there I was asking myself... What am I working to go get now? I stood there staring at the mirror and saw that I had a wealth of experience, a stellar reputation in the industry, and for the first time in my life I had a bit of extra capital to not have to get another job (thankfully). However, I realized that I had sold the one thing that mattered to me the most: my purpose that brought me fulfillment.

I wasn't quite ready to start another SaaS company – and to be honest, I was a little burnt out from it. But at the same time, I wasn't quite ready to just go to Ibiza and check out yet. Not quite exactly sure what else to do besides start a company, I turned to the tools I had acquired through my startup journey to get clarity on what I wanted out of this next chapter of my life. Very quickly, and almost accidentally, the process I followed for over a decade to unlock some of my wildest goals and gain clarity into my life became the same process I turned to craft a new vision of fulfillment for this next chapter in my life. Instead of going to Ibiza, I bet it all. I bet all of the money I made on a new venture called Unstoppable.

Today at the time of this writing, Unstoppable is a strategic advisory firm that serves 250+ SaaS CEOs & Founders globally to help them craft and execute on an unstoppable strategy for their life and their business. But when I first started, I'll be honest – Unstoppable was just an idea. It started as a phrase and mantra I kept telling to myself when I navigated through some of the toughest times in the companies I worked in. It was a set of skills I had to learn to survive and then thrive. And it was a set of principles that never came in an instruction manual.

All I knew was that I wanted to create the "missing instruction manual for CEOs and Founders." As I reflected on my journey, I saw that through my ups and downs of my startup journey as a bootstrapped Founder, then a Venture Backed Founder, then a high performance executive at the age of 34, and having worked at the best hedge fund in the world (Bridgewater), raised from the best venture capital firm in the world (Andreessen Horowitz), and even having worked at a company owned by the best SaaS private equity firm in the world (Vista) – through all of this -- I went through a wealth of learning lessons that should've come in an instruction manual. But here's the thing: VC checks don't come with an instruction manual. And I knew there was something there.

I had no idea what the "missing instruction manual for CEOs and Founders" would be... but that was okay, it felt familiar. Why? Because the vision felt right, even though the implementation wasn't quite obvious. It reminded me of the early days of starting any of my prior companies, it gave me that feeling of "This could be huge" - a feeling that I never thought I'd be able to get back to again. It was a glimmer of hope for finding fulfillment again.

Fast forward the past few years since publishing the 1st edition of this book, the vision for Unstoppable and delivering that missing instruction manual has come to life. It started small, much like most things that become big. It started with me writing the 1st edition of this book on How to Live a Proactive Life (because I learned that CEOs and Founders who ran their personal lives well ran their businesses even better). The book sold thousands of copies to Founders, CEOs, aspiring Entrepreneurs, and even people who never wanted to start a company but knew they wanted "more" from their life. The next step to the book became our Unstoppable Life (https://getunstoppable.com/life) program where we brought together an online community of like minded Unstoppable people and gave them step-by-step training on how to implement all the principles you'll read in this book.

But then something crazy happened. A number of the Founders who were part of Unstoppable told me "Hey look. This is great. I'm getting so much value from this. But can you help us with scaling our SaaS companies?"

The one thing I learned in my own startup journey is this: "You don't find Product Market Fit. Instead, Product Market Fit finds you." So I decided to give them what they wanted. I built the next thing: the missing instruction manual for scaling SaaS companies. We started our flagship SaaS GTM Program (https://getunstoppable.com/gtm) where we taught these same Founders how to build and execute on an unstoppable strategy for their business. To augment the book, and the programs, I doubled down on my Youtube channel where every week I shared parts of the missing instruction manual on building an unstoppable strategy for your life and business.

Little by little, that vision of creating the "missing instruction manual" turned into thousands of copies sold of this book and becoming an International Amazon Best Seller, it expanded into my Youtube channel (https://getunstoppable.com/youtube) which is now one of the fastest growing channels for SaaS Founders and CEOs on how to build an unstoppable strategy for their life and business. And... It turned into our SaaS Go-To-Market Program for driving to $3M in ARR, and then the SaaS Strategy Program (https://getunstoppable.com/scale) where we work with CEOs upwards of $100M+ (and growing) to scale SaaS companies.

In the blink of an eye, or at least what seems that way now... I had found my fulfillment. Serving a global legion of Unstoppable SaaS CEOs, Unstoppable CxO Leaders, and even Unstoppable Talent (https://getunstoppable.com/talent) to unlock their wildest goals in their personal and professional lives with the power of an Unstoppable strategy.

Did it take hard work? Yes. Were there moments where I struggled? Absolutely. Am I perfect now? Absolutely not. But it came together. And it came together for thousands of others who have applied these principles in the book to adopt the Unstoppable ethos.

Thanks to the tools that you'll read about in this book, I was once again able to pause and reflect on my life, craft a strategy and vision for my personal life, and execute with belief x discipline. In that journey, Unstoppable became Unstoppable, and I became Unstoppable.

Let me be clear. Unstoppable doesn't mean that you're perfect. It means that you have complete clarity in what you want out of life and you're constantly operating in a proactive way to pursue that goal despite the inevitable road bumps. And it means you never feel the Sunday jitters and instead you go into every single Monday with complete clarity on the task and goals at hand. That's what Unstoppable was to me when I first murmured that mantra to myself in tough situations while running my companies (and there were plenty). That's what Unstoppable is to our global legion of Unstoppable people.

So why a 2nd edition? Why now? I've learned over the past few years that the way I study the game is by teaching it. That's what allows me to play the game and win over and over. When I wrote the first edition years ago, I really just wrote the book for myself. I was following my process to craft an unstoppable strategy and I knew that if I taught others to do the same – I'd do a 10x better job of doing it for myself. And I hoped that it would be the beginning of that "missing instruction manual."

But this time around, after seeing it work so well for so many people, I knew this book deserved a second turn, a revamped version, based on everything we have learned in implementing these principles. And therein lies the impetus for this 2nd edition.

The principles in this book work. Not just for me. But for all of us in the legion. Trust in the process, and let's get to it. I'm excited for you. Here's to you becoming Unstoppable.

ACKNOWLEDGMENTS

Thank you to Sabera Kader and Tawfiq Kader, my parents, who have always encouraged me to pursue my dreams and aim for the stars.

For giving me an unbelievable decade of opportunities, growth, life long friendships and for helping me find my own unstoppability through thick and thin, thank you to the ToutApp team and the Marketo team.

For encouraging me even before I believed in myself that I had a book in me and that I should dedicate my life's purpose to helping people become Unstoppable, thank you to my brother Shahed Kader, and my dear friends Lin Fox and Adria Hou.

For helping me through countless edits of this book, for encouraging me every step of the way with comments of positivity inside our shared Google document, a special thank you to Ali Mazzotta and Janean Laidlaw. For helping me craft, edit, and publish the 2nd Edition of this book, a special thank you to Islam Obeidat.

And most importantly, thank you to the Unstoppable community and the incredible SaaS Founders, CEOs and Leaders I have the honor and privilege to serve. You inspire me.

INTRODUCTION:
HOW TO GET PROACTIVE ABOUT YOUR LIFE AND BECOME UNSTOPPABLE

In this book, I will help you escape the Sunday Jitters by showing you how to lead a more proactive life instead of just reacting to things that come at you. This will allow you to become a high-performance person living a proactive life and guide you in accomplishing some of your wildest goals that may seem beyond your reach but deep down inside you know you're capable of and deserve to unlock.

I'll start by helping you punch the Sunday Jitters in the face by teaching you a practice called Unstoppable Sundays, a practice that has unlocked a decade of productivity and unparalleled success in my own life. It'll help you take stock of where you are and get more proactive about the next seven days of your life. Then I'll help you look ahead to the next 365 days and set clear priorities across key areas of your life. Once we've got a good handle on your NOW and immediate future, I'll walk you through setting a vision for yourself for the next five years so that you can start to become the best version of yourself, one Unstoppable Sunday at a time. By the end of this book, you'll have adopted the habits of a high-performance person, you'll have a clear life plan in place, and you'll be able to execute with certainty.

I've made this book only as long as it needs to be. I wrote it all myself without the use of a single ghost writer and I've made this book as actionable as possible so that you can get to DOING versus just READING and DREAMING about that proactive life we all deeply desire. And, most importantly, this book is based on the system I have developed for myself: a system that has unlocked nearly a decade of productivity and success for my own personal and professional life.

The truth is, I wasn't always like this. I had Sundays, just like you, where I felt that pit in my stomach. Call it the Sunday Scaries, the Sunday angst, or the Sunday existential "What am I even doing with my life?!" I've been there -- and I took the time to read all the books and to research the best ways to break out of it. And I did it.

If I could break down my life into parts, I would describe two distinct phases: the BEFORE and the AFTER.

The BEFORE was when I ran around like a madman, frantic -- trying to eke out every single second I could find toward my work. I'd wake up in the morning, and, with my phone in hand, I'd be brushing my teeth, wrangling on my pants, answering email -- basically all at once. It wasn't pretty.

And then there's the AFTER. The AFTER is when I wake up slowly. I brush my teeth. I meditate. All before I even think of picking up my phone. I make time for family and friends. I put in a solid set of hours toward my most important goals, and I take breaks. I pause and reflect on Sundays to check in on my goals; and I constantly adapt to take on and conquer bigger challenges in my life.

GUESS which part of my life yielded my best work? The best results? GUESS which part of my life led to the happiest moments, the BIGGEST wins, and the deepest lessons learned?!?

Yeah, obviously. It was the latter part.

I learned (almost too late) in my life that taking a PROACTIVE approach to my days led to a calmer me. A less frantic me.

Why do we become so frantic? It's not because we do our best work when we're frenzied... It's because, deep down, we have no way of checking in and understanding if we're on track. It's because no matter how many hours we work, we don't feel like we're enough and our work is enough.

That all changed when I developed a simple system to check in on myself every Sunday to get rid of the angst I felt every Sunday afternoon, as I thought about Monday. Even today, EVERY Sunday, I still sit down, I open a Word document, and I answer two simple questions:

1) Where am I?
2) What do I do next?

This simple ritual allows me to consistently check in on my goals, check in on my progress, and, MOST IMPORTANTLY, it allows me to course correct.

This simple ritual became a critical part of a whole system I developed to take control of every day of my life, to be proactive about life, and, most importantly, to eradicate the angst I used to feel in my stomach every Sunday night about the week that was to come.

If you feel like there just isn't enough time in the day for you, your loved ones, and your work... If you're feeling constantly behind... Then this book that I created to help you plan out your life and become PROACTIVE, is for you.

The Japanese embrace a concept called "Kaizen," which I love. The direct English translation is "Continuous Improvement." It's a strategy whereby you work proactively to achieve regular and incremental improvements to a process (in this case: how you live your life). In a sense, Kaizen combines the collective resources at your disposal (your time, your energy, your intellect, your mentors, your friends) to create a powerful engine for improvement in your own life.

This book is not designed to give you a one-and-done "workshop" in figuring out your life's purpose. Figuring out what you want from life and the steps to realize that dream can be a lifelong journey. This book helps you establish an iterative process through which you can switch from being a reactive person to a proactive person, and helps you establish the systems that you can follow for the rest of your life to continue to improve your life.

In this book, I'll walk you through a set of tools, processes, and systems that all work together to allow you to practice the art of Kaizen for your own life's purpose. By following this system, you'll be able to achieve clarity of vision for yourself, set goals for yourself, and create a plan of purposeful and focused action for yourself that you consistently improve upon as you execute your plan. Most importantly, this will help you set an agenda that YOU choose for your life.

I've used this system for nearly a decade and it has unlocked unparalleled levels of productivity and wealth for me, personally. In the little less than a year since I open-sourced this system, thousands of people have downloaded our Unstoppable Proactive Life Planning Guide. All of this led to the publishing of the book you are reading right now.

When you think of your life in terms of Kaizen -- in terms of a continuous improvement process backed by powerful self-reflection -- everything changes. As you learn more by following this book, you'll continue to iterate on your goals and plans. As you make mistakes, you'll course-correct from lessons learned. And as you unlock new levels of success, you'll continue to set new goals that take you to the next level.

In the following chapters, I'll introduce key ideas to help you create a plan for yourself and to continuously improve upon it:

- **In Chapters 1 through 3**, I'll introduce you to the core principles of Dreaming, Belief and Discipline that makes for a proactive life. I'll also dive into what separates the DABBLERS from the DO-ERS and why visualizing the STATUS QUO of your life will help you conceptualize why changing the trajectory of your life is a MUST.
- **In Chapter 4,** I'll introduce you to the concept of a 45-Day challenge. A tool that I've used in my life over and over again to drive focused and purposeful change in my life in an easy way.
- **In Chapter 5,** I introduce you to the idea of practicing Unstoppable Sundays: We'll teach you to reflect on and plan for the next seven days so that you can eradicate the Sunday Scaries and get proactive about the week ahead...
- **In Chapter 6,** I help you zoom out and start to think about your one-year plan by answering a set of very pointed questions that help you

to practice gratitude, to assess where you are today, and to then start laying out a plan for your next 365 days.

- **In Chapter 7,** I introduce a new tool that you can use to become proactive about the 365 days you are given every year, so that you can be proactive about how you spend your days and months in a given year, and you will be able to make tough trade-offs on what you spend your time on versus not -- ahead of time, instead of two weeks before Thanksgiving.
- **In Chapter 8,** now that you have established an understanding of where you are in your current situation (next seven days; next 365 days), in this chapter we help you really zoom out, think big, and think about the next five years of your life and the vision you want to set for yourself.
- **In Chapter 9,** I walk you through the most significant impediment you face in your life in achieving your goals, and how you can overcome it by making one simple change. (hint: It's all about the law of averages.)
- **In Chapter 10,** the closing chapter, I wrap it all together and walk you through how you can now start to use the tools and follow the systems we gave you and practice the art of being proactive in your life. We teach you the reminders you will need to set on your calendar in order to make sure you continue to iterate on your life plan and become Unstoppable in life.

If you have the **Belief** that what you desire is possible and achievable, and if you have the **Discipline** to pursue that Belief with focused and purposeful action, regardless of the roadblocks that you encounter -- you will be Unstoppable.

Let's get started. Let's go create your life plan. Let's go make you Unstoppable.

belief x **discipline** makes you **Unstoppable**

TABLE OF CONTENTS

CHAPTER 1:

WHAT SETS APART THOSE WHO DREAM FROM THOSE WHO ARE SUCCESSFUL?

"Whether you think you can,
or you think you can't — you're right."
— Henry Ford

An unbelievable 53% of millennials expect to become millionaires during their lifetime. Before you chuckle and scoff "MILLENNIALS" -- it's not just millennials who dream big: 29% of all Americans believe they will become millionaires. Young people dream big about their lives and have high expectations around living the life they desire, but this motivation simply drops off over time.

This dream is not about just becoming financially wealthy. It's about any big and crazy goal that you have -- whether it is to graduate college, start your own business, land that dream job, or become a star athlete. What I'm talking about is becoming exceptional by your own definition.

On one hand, you have dreamers; and then, on the other hand, you have those who actually figure out how to make their dreams a reality. What is the difference between these two groups of people? What is the difference between the DREAMERS and the DABBLERS versus the DO-ERS? Regardless of where you are in life, or your age, you have a choice to make as you read this book: Which group will you belong to from this day forward?

When you look at anyone who has achieved massive success in their lives, whether it is the captains of industry or the stealthy next-door millionaires, you will see that they have all learned to master two key principles in their life: Belief and Discipline.

Dreaming is a beautiful thing. It allows us to imagine what is possible in our lives. We dream freely as children, less so in our teenage years, and we seem to stop dreaming when we become adults -- instead succumbing to what life has dealt us. Somehow, we call this "growing up." Little by little, we get used to accepting crumbs. Dreaming coupled with Belief and Discipline, on the other hand, enables us to take charge when it comes to our goals, so they can become reality.

Somehow, dreaming is easy for us when we are children; yet as we get older, there are fewer of us who dare to dream. And even fewer of us actually accomplish those dreams. This book will give you the tools necessary to dare to dream and turn those dreams into reality.

The formula to accomplish the things we want in our life is simple. You **dream**, you **believe** in that dream, and then you follow through with **discipline** to accomplish that dream. Then, you dream bigger. Rinse and repeat. You revel in the journey and celebrate the wins. In this chapter, I'll walk you through why it is important to adopt all three of those components, particularly Belief and Discipline, so that you can set yourself apart and be one of the few who actually realizes your dreams.

Dreaming is the most idle state of thinking about the life that you want. It's important to understand that it is only the first step to actually achieving the life we want. We dream when we scroll through Instagram and look at a picture of that beautiful kitchen we desire, the fancy sports car we want to drive, that laptop lifestyle traveling the world while we do what we love, or even that big house in the perfect cul-de-sac. It's empty calories. It makes

4

you feel better, it makes you dream "one day..." but it doesn't actually change a thing about your reality.

Believing, on the other hand, is the active state of truly conceptualizing that what you desire is possible and that it can and will happen for you. Believing gets you to commit that you want to make that dream a reality. Furthermore, taking disciplined and purposeful action on that belief turns that belief into actual reality.

You have a decision to make. When I wrote this book, my goal was simple: Give people an actionable framework to help turn their dreams into reality, to turn their lives into the lives they deserve, regardless of their circumstances. But this book won't do it for you; the framework won't do it for you. There is no quick win or fix here. Only you, through applying the actionable framework laid out in the latter chapters of this book, can turn your dreams into reality. And it is done through two simple ideas that you must adopt into your life: Belief and Discipline.

How to Get Belief

The dictionary definition of Belief is simple enough: "an acceptance that a statement is true or that something exists."

What is your dream for your life? You purchased this book because of one simple reason: You know deep down inside that there is more you want out of your life. Your days. Your weeks.

When I was 16, I was an immigrant kid born in Bangladesh and living in Queens, New York in a one-bedroom apartment with six people in all. My father worked seven days a week. My mother supported the family and the business. We all pitched in any way we could in order to achieve the American Dream and make a better life for ourselves in New York. I started working for the family business at age 12, handing out flyers for our business at the corner of 74th Street and 37th Avenue -- partly because I just wanted to spend more time with my dad, and partly because I had big dreams even then for myself and my family, and I wanted to do everything that was in my power to have an impact.

I pledged to have a bigger dream as I turned 16. I pledged that I'd grind hard through my 20s so that I could get to a life where I could provide not just for myself, but also for my parents and for my future family. And no, my dream wasn't just about living and providing, but it was to get to a life where I had the wealth to do whatever I wanted with my time, to shape the world and leave it better than I found it. I considered it not only my dream but my duty.

What is the dream for your life? Your dream could be one of these:

I am going to have control over my life and spend my time the way I want to.

I am going to spend my days working on what I love.

I am going to provide for my family so that we have more than enough.

This book is not meant to be a piece of art that sits on your bookshelf or one that just gets forgotten.

So grab a pen, and start writing into this book as you go through these chapters. This book will transform into a roadmap for your life and a physical reminder of your commitment to become Unstoppable in life.

Or perhaps you'd describe it differently. Go ahead write it down here:

How do you get from dreaming to true Belief? Some personal development experts would say you need to get up and scream out your dream and yell out "I BELIEVE!" That may feel energetic and fulfilling for a moment, but will it truly get your whole body to commit and believe?

Probably. But will it bring you the lasting change you need to make your dream a reality? It didn't work for me.

The quickest and fastest and most effective way I found to believe in my dreams was to seek out role models who had achieved similar dreams. I didn't have to know them personally; I just needed to know that it's possible.

There's something that shifts within us when we see that something is possible. For me, it always brought forward a feeling of: "Well... if HE can do it... then I surely can pull it off..."

This led me to go through the mental process of actually articulating my dream, what it means to me, and of convincing myself that this doesn't just have to be a dream but that it can be my reality.

When it comes to Belief, the person most known for profoundly turning a dream into reality through a strongly held belief is Roger Bannister. Bannister's legend was born on May 6, 1954, when he became the first man on this planet to run a mile in under four minutes – a feat that scientists of that day simply deemed impossible and perhaps even deadly to the human body.

It had never been done before. And this was 1954 -- man was hardly new to running at that time! And yet, within two months of Bannister's accomplishing the first four-minute mile, John Landy and Roger Bannister each ran a four-minute-mile again. Just a year later, three runners broke the four-minute barrier again, in just a single race. In 1964, Jim Ryun became the first high-school runner to break the four-minute mile.

According to the Harvard Business Review, runners had been seriously chasing the four-minute mile record since at least 1886. After Roger Bannister, over the last half-century, more than 1,300 runners have overcome the challenge of running a mile in under four minutes -- one that had been considered hopelessly out of reach.

What changed? Did humans all of a sudden evolve quickly to become four-minute-mile runners? No. Did they cheat and use drugs to achieve new heights? No. What changed was the belief that running a four-minute mile is indeed possible. Once the limit was broken by one athlete, others thought as much as I did: "Well if ROGER can do it..." They all believed.

Belief helped me grow my career as a computer engineer. Belief helped me start my own company and grow it into a multi-million-dollar business as a startup CEO at 28 years old. Belief helped me become a millionaire and achieve enough financially by my 30s so that I could provide for my family. More importantly, Belief helped me get to a point where I can spend my time on movements like Unstoppable to help people lead more proactive lives, something I am deeply passionate about. That's the dream I had at 16.

If you want to bring lasting change into your life, you have to get serious about your beliefs. And even more importantly, you have to pause and reflect, to understand if there are conflicting beliefs in your life that are stopping you from achieving your dream.

How to Get Discipline

At age 16, I believed I would be 30 by the time I would be able to get to a point where I could do whatever I want. That dream of "Do whatever I want..." was still alive and well for me as age 30 approached, especially for an immigrant kid who had always had a to-do list of things "I must do so that I can..." get to what I wanted to do. I was willing to dream it, believe it. I was willing to take risks to get it. But in fact, I was far from it as 30 approached.

I had a deep belief in what I wanted to accomplish in my life. I had connected with the people who had done it before and had studied them closely. What am I doing wrong?! I thought to myself... It wasn't adding up.

I had gotten good at pausing and reflecting. I had gotten great at visualizing the things that I wanted. I even took risks, like quitting my six-figure finance job and starting my own company. I had even had success already, and my software company was just starting to do well with employees, an office and amazing customers.

Truth is, by the time I turned 30, I had developed only half of the Unstoppable Life system that I talk about in this book. The word Unstoppable hadn't even entered my psyche yet. There was a critical component that was still missing in my life: Discipline.

Having Belief, true Belief, in what you want, gets you to start taking real action -- as I had in my life. But that is only half of the equation. At age 30, I was working 90-hour weeks. I was burnt out. I was waking up every morning and jumping right at it every single day. But this was still that "BEFORE" in my life. I hadn't yet mastered Discipline.

Before Roger Bannister broke the four-minute-mile record, he failed countless times at achieving that goal. Before he set his sights on that goal, he failed at earning a medal while competing in the Olympics. It is the story since the beginning of time of a person who has experienced "overnight" success: It took years of hard work, mistakes, overcoming obstacles, and life lessons to get to that moment of "success."

At that moment as I tried to figure out "What am I missing?!" I realized two critical things that rounded out my beliefs regarding an Unstoppable life:

1) The biggest lie we are ever told in our life is that we get to a point where there are no more problems in our lives. Truth is, there are always going to be good days and bad days, problems and challenges. The key to living an Unstoppable life is embracing this truism but committing to solve BIGGER problems that have BIGGER rewards, every single day, and determination to grow so much stronger that yesterday's problems seem like an inconvenient speed bump.

2) The road to success is a marathon and not a sprint, and is riddled with setbacks and speed bumps, and only those who take definitive and smart action and who have staying power actually get to realize their dreams. This is where Discipline comes in.

I could've given up at 30. I could've said "This isn't working. Maybe my dream is too big, maybe it isn't achievable." Instead, I doubled down on my Belief and strived to understand what I was missing. I mastered Discipline.

And at age 31, I accomplished one of the early stages of my dream. We grew the company to a critical inflection point which allowed us to raise a large round of investment from a venture capital firm.

If it weren't for Discipline, I wouldn't have gotten there. As I look back, it is truly frightening to realize that I was so close to giving up just moments before accomplishing my dream.

Discipline is:

- Treating life like a marathon that we are running, instead of a sprint where we hold our breath until we get to this mythical finish line where all our problems go away. Treating life like a marathon where we get better and better in all aspects of our life, instead of a sprint where we forsake love, health, and just about everything else, just to reach a point of success that may not taste as sweet as we think.

- Recognizing that in order to win this marathon, we have to learn to have Discipline today so that we will not experience regret tomorrow. It means that we must prioritize the right things while tending to all the important things. It means that we have to master the art of consistency in the daily actions that allow us to run the marathon.

- Most importantly, Discipline is the art of constantly keeping our bigger goals crystal-clear in our mind, taking purposeful action consistently every day, while remembering to enjoy the moment instead of holding our breath only for the reward at the end.

Roger Bannister kept failing. But he mastered the art of Discipline and doubled down on his Belief to finally break the four-minute--mile barrier. Shortly after he did so, many other athletes followed.

There's a famous saying that originated with Persian Sufi Poets and that has been repeated across religions and philosophies, and has even been used by great orators like Abraham Lincoln: THIS TOO SHALL PASS.

This is one of my most favorite mantras in life, particularly in my quest to become Unstoppable, because it reminds me of a simple idea. If I'm having the best day of my life, this too shall pass. If I'm having the worst day of my life, this too shall also pass. It reminds us of the impermanence

of the moments in our lives and of the "status" that we seek in our lives. It'll all pass.

So, I choose to smile and constantly practice Discipline through the bad times, even at age 30. In the moments when we are celebrating a win, I smile and revel in the moment, because I know this will pass. In the moments when I'm facing adversity and pain and fear, I still smile, because I appreciate the impermanence of this situation and know that I have the tools in front of me to go punch the adversity in the face.

That mantra led me to rely on another favorite mantra of mine, one I learned when I was working for Ray Dalio at Bridgewater Associates, a famed

hedge fund investor and the author of the book PRINCIPLES. Whenever we

found ourselves facing a difficult situation or a complex challenge, he'd

always remind us: THESE ARE JUST PROBLEMS. PROBLEMS HAVE SOLUTIONS.

Much as we were trained early in life to think we have to work to get to a point where we are "happy" and have zero problems, the same people lied to us and taught us to buckle down and crumble in the face of problems.

Ray always reminded us, "Look, these are just problems. Nothing more, nothing less. All problems have solutions. It's up to you, your creativity, your intellect, and your power, to find the solution (usually just one of many) to overcome the problem you are facing. All problems have solutions."

How to Apply Belief x Discipline

In order to become Unstoppable in life, you must realize two things.

First, you must realize what Unstoppable is not. It is not about being perfect or achieving perfection. It is not about having all the answers. It is not about flawless execution of your goals. It is going after big lofty goals that inspire us and motivate us, and about expecting there to be speed bumps, problems, challenges, and obstacles along the way. It is about expecting those things to happen, but having the conviction, mindset and wherewithal to know that no matter what bumps appear in the road, we will find a way to get past them. There will be problems. But all problems have solutions. You are Unstoppable when you find a way to forge ahead with a smile, regardless of the road bumps.

Second, you must become great at practicing Dreaming, Belief and Discipline. Dreaming big and having high expectations of yourself and your life. Belief that what you desire and what you imagine in your head is possible for you, and that one day you will achieve it. Discipline in taking the focused and purposeful action every single day to run the marathon and conquer it.

Belief multiplied by Discipline (Belief x Discipline) became an Unstoppable force in my life. Once I developed this mindset, my life became an Unstoppable screaming freight train from hell that put me on an unrelenting path toward crushing one goal after another. That's what I want for you and your life.

With my simple mantra of Belief x Discipline, I found a way to evolve from being just a dreamer into being a person who actually realizes my dreams. You can too.

Chapter 1,
Questions to Ask Yourself

What is it that you desire from your life that you are afraid of admitting to anyone else?

What are the things "you don't know how to do" that are holding you back from achieving your biggest dream of your life?

Nothing overcomes speed bumps and obstacles better than focused and purposeful action. What kind of daily disciplines, weekly disciplines, even monthly disciplines can you adopt to break through these "Don't KNOWs" in your life?

You're likely in a space right now where you're feeling PUMPED and HOPEFUL about the future. Let's take this moment to practice a quick Unstoppable Sunday (even if right NOW is not a Sunday) together. Just to see how it feels and get you going.

Where am I? What am I feeling?

What do I do next?

Chapter 1,
Actions to Take

☐ As you go through your days, start taking stock of the deeply-held beliefs that you constantly reinforce within yourself (good or bad). Write these down on your phone's Notes application if this makes it easy for you to keep track. What're the things you are telling yourself that are stopping you from believing what you can achieve?

☐ In later chapters, we'll start to help you create a new, consistent Discipline for yourself. For now, start to take note of how you spend your days. What do you do when you wake up? What are your routines for the days? How do you like to spend your weekends? As you work through the next few chapters, you'll start to go through exercises that help you pick and choose the Disciplines that help you to get closer to your goals, and to cut out the ones that do not.

CHAPTER 2:
UPPER LIMITING AND FEAR OF SUCCESS

"Success requires no apologies.
Failure permits no alibis."
— Napoleon Hill

For a major part of my life, I had a fear of success. Early on in life, I wasn't even aware of such a concept. Once I did find out about it, I at first denied having it, and then it took me years to really grapple with and deal with my fear of success. Before I truly dealt with it, I stumbled through small amounts of success through sheer willpower -- simply because I wanted it bad enough. Once I dealt with it, I unlocked years upon years of success for myself across my personal and business life.

If one of us were to have a bullet wound in the chest and to be bleeding, people would recognize it right away; we would feel the pain right away; and the entire world around us would come together to help us heal the wound. Immediately.

Unfortunately, we and the world surrounding us are not likewise equipped to deal with deep-rooted issues like fear of success. And although as a society we've grown by leaps and bounds to recognize mental health issues such as depression, the deep programming we have within us around success, money, motivation, and beliefs is nearly impossible to spot unless we ourselves take time to look within.

Back in 2012, my company, ToutApp, was a four-person company. We had raised a little bit of money; we created software that people loved; and it was generating revenue. Much like the early days of a startup, there were glimmers of hope, and early traction, but I was stuck. I knew I wanted more from my business, but I just couldn't get myself to move forward. I felt like someone who was running forward, but there was an invisible hand holding me back no matter how hard I worked and no matter how much harder I pushed forward.

I just told myself... "This is supposed to be hard. I'm supposed to hustle. I just need to put in more hours. More time. More effort. More energy. More, more, more... Nothing huge comes easy."

And yet... as if there was a thermostat set inside of me for my success to be at a four-person company, no matter how much cold air I blew into the room through momentous effort, the internal thermostat kicked in and just neutralized the effort, keeping the company at four people.

I had already adopted the things I teach in this book. I dreamt. I believed in my vision of creating a thriving software company. I paused and reflected every Sunday. I visualized how one day I'd walk into a huge office and it would be packed with people buzzing away at serving our customers and building features I had only dreamed of. And yet... we were stuck at four people.

I knew something was wrong, but I couldn't figure out what. And so I did what I did every time I hit a roadblock. I started reading books on being stuck. I started googling about feeling stuck. Eventually I came across the concept of limiting beliefs, upper limiting, and fear of success.

I then came across an exercise that changed my life. The exercise was simple. It was a set of questions that walked me through to an understanding of my core fear and of what exactly was the limiting belief that was holding me back.

It first asked: What do you want?

I want my software company to thrive. I want to have a hundred employees working for me so that we can serve more people, have more customers, make more money, and turn ToutApp into a revenue-generating machine.

It then asked: What would you have to do to get what you want?

I knew exactly what I had to do. We had to make our current customers successful. We had to expand our feature set, uplevel our messaging, become more aggressive about getting our word out, and, most importantly, we had to expand our sales capacity so we could sell more.

I knew the answers! What was holding me back, I wondered?

Surely enough, it then asked: *What could go wrong if you did those things?*
I felt a knot in my stomach.

> *The software might not scale.*

> *We might hire people who may not be good at what they do.*

> *We might have to hire WAY MORE people, and then I'd have to manage all of them!*

> *We might run out of money. We might find out that our software is not great and the broader market doesn't want it.*

We would have to find a way to support all those customers.

We would have to find a way to educate all these customers on how to use the software, and that might be harder to do for mass adoption versus for the early adopters we have now.

Competitors might start copying us, and then we'd lose our position in the market and get trumped.

I may not be good enough to build a software that so many people would want!

The list went on... Within minutes, I had listed a full page of things that would go horribly wrong if we were to become successful. It was a wake-up call for me. There I was, toiling away, my team was toiling away, and yet all of these things were subconsciously pulling me back from achieving success -- because I was afraid of all the things I would have to deal with if we were successful!

The exercise was unrelenting and unapologetic. It then asked: *You're now successful. Those problems that are your demons are now real. How would you overcome those problems, given your newfound success?*

As you might imagine: I had an answer for every single problem I was deeply afraid of.

More customers meant more revenues, meant more dry powder.

More customers, more revenue, meant more employees who could help solve problems.

More growth meant more investment dollars coming in.

More revenues and more investment dollars meant I could hire smarter people to solve problems and help manage more employees.

The exercise then asked: *If you are NOT successful, what would happen?*

Death. I answered. *We would die, we would fail, it wouldn't matter anyway.*

It then asked: *If you ARE successful, what are the positive things that would happen?*

I would thrive. My employees would thrive. We could deliver MORE for our customers. Our customers would thrive. It would be WIN-WIN-WIN for everyone involved. Our wildest dreams could come true and all our effort would be WORTH IT.

The exercise finished with... *What're you waiting for?*

What was I waiting for?! What was I afraid of?! The worst-case scenario was our failure, which was assured if we didn't do the things necessary to achieve success anyway.

By the middle of 2012, shortly after I completed this exercise, we doubled the number of employees to a whopping eight people on a single day.

By the end of 2012, we sold so much software, we did a pre-emptive Series A round of $3.3m from Jackson Square Ventures to help support and accelerate our growth.

Through 2013, we grew the company 300% in a single year, increased to 40 employees, and raised another $15m from Andreessen Horowitz.

Through 2015, we grew the company again, to nearly 80 people, and through twists and turns (which I'll leave for another time) we sold the company in 2017 to Marketo, a market leader in the space.

The exercise made me realize two important things about living a proactive life:

1. Without doing the basics, such as setting goals, practicing Belief and Discipline, and having a sense of urgency, failure is guaranteed.

2. However, even with doing those things, we may be walking around with subconscious programming in our minds because of our environment or upbringing that may sabotage our own success.

It's unbelievable, isn't it? We could be working tirelessly toward our goals, could wholeheartedly want to be successful, and yet our subconscious programming could be actively working AGAINST us to sabotage our forward momentum. When I felt like I was pushing ahead but there was an imaginary hand pushing back against forward momentum, I wasn't wrong. I felt the right thing! The "hand" was my own fear of success, it was my feeling like I didn't deserve success. It was my feeling that I wasn't enough.

What are the limiting beliefs and fears that are holding you back from your path to success?

Was it being taught at an early age that money is evil? Is it a fear of all the bigger problems you'll have to solve tomorrow if you are successful today? Is it the memory of your parents telling you at an early age that you're not good enough or doing something wrong? Is it friends or a significant other who is unsupportive of your dreams?

We all have these things in our life. It's just that we're not trained to identify these negative patterns in our lives as they work silently in the background to sabotage our hard work.

Now, I don't mind failing because I got the market trends wrong. Or because I miscalculated a strategic move. Or I made a poor business decision. I can own that. I can learn from that. I can come back stronger than ever from that. But to sabotage myself because of my own fears? That is simply **unacceptable**.

Throughout the rest of this book, I will help you craft a life strategy and a proactive plan. But before we delve into that, I want you to follow the same exercise that I followed, in order to identify the subconscious fears deviously holding you back from the life you deserve.

Chapter 2,
Questions to Ask Yourself

What are you actively working on right now toward achieving in your life?

What would you have to do to get what you want?

What could go wrong if you did those things and were successful? How would it complicate your life?

You're now successful. Those problems that are your demons are now real. How would you overcome those problems, given your newfound success?

If you are NOT successful, you maintain the status quo and don't grow, what would happen?

If you ARE successful, what are the positive things that would happen?

What're you waiting for? What are the immediate steps you can take now to move forward?

Chapter 2,
Actions to Take

☐ Go talk to a loved one or a best friend about what you've discovered in this chapter. See if he or she, too, has fears of success and compare notes.

☐ You're doing great. Keep going!

CHAPTER 3:
WHAT DOES THE STATUS QUO LOOK LIKE FOR YOU?

*"The riskiest thing we can do is
maintain the status quo"*

— Bob Iger

A two-year study by the McKinsey Global Institute found that by 2030, intelligent agents and robots could eliminate as much as 30 percent of the world's human labor. That is an estimated 800 million jobs done better, faster, and more precisely by robots in the place of humans.

The fear that machines will replace human labor has been an existential fear dating back to the Luddites in the early 19th century. Regardless of whether you believe the end of humans in jobs is a groundless fear or is a real threat, there is one undeniable fact: The rate of change in how our world works and how to earn a decent living is rapidly changing and will deeply impact each of us and our families in our lifetime.

This begs the question: If the world is changing, and if you do not change, what does the rest of your lifetime look like for you? If you maintain your status quo, what is the trajectory of your life?

I faced such a question as I was at the supposed peak of my career at age 25, sitting in my own office, at the largest and most successful hedge fund in the world. I looked around for role models, and I asked myself: If I continue on this trajectory, if I live life the same way I am living now, who will I become ten years from now? What will the end of my life look like?

Most 25-year-olds don't think this way. We feel limitless and hopeful at age 25, and we think and dream that anything is possible. However, I had recently come across a quotation that had me thinking about this deeply:

"What is the definition of Hell? On your last day on Earth, the person you became will meet the person you could have become."

That quotation struck me, not because I felt scared by it. I don't feel scared by the changing world, I don't feel scared by robots, or some existential threat, and I don't bring this up in this chapter to scare you, either.

It struck me because it made me stop, pause, and wonder. It made me wonder: What am I capable of?

What's the absolute BEST version of myself that I can become?

In my wildest dreams, with my most earnest effort, with focus, discipline, and belief, what am I capable of becoming?

What impact am I capable of having on this world?

What would that mean for me and my family?

And, most importantly: Am I living my life and spending my days on a trajectory that sets me up to achieve that greatness?

Greatness is an interesting word. I believe we're all capable of our own definition of greatness, not society's expectation or definition of greatness, but mine.

It made me think: What is my version of greatness?

If I've lived my life, and I look back, what are the things I will have regretted not trying or not doing?

What are the things I am spending time on today that are in conflict with my definition of, vision of, and aspiration toward, greatness?

What are the things you are spending your time on today that are in conflict with your definition of greatness?

Greatness to me means that I leave the world better than I found it. Greatness to me means that I become a better version of myself every single day, and that I am able not only to provide for my family and loved ones, but that I am able to reach a plane of success where I can do what matters.

What is your definition of greatness for yourself? What is your vision of your life over a 50-year period? Not tomorrow, not this very minute, but if you take a step back and really close your eyes and imagine what it is you are capable of and what you want to become over a FIFTY-YEAR period... What is that?

As I sat in my office at the largest hedge fund in the world, with all sorts of creature comforts around me, and people even more successful than I running around, I thought to myself: Will this path take me to greatness?

I didn't have the answers to any of this. But in that moment, I had a lot to think about.

Fortunately for me, Bridgewater Associates, at that time, and even today, was a culture and a place that encouraged this type of introspection. We were encouraged to think about and define our core values, our strengths, and our weaknesses -- not at a superficial, corporate level, but at a deep, human level. I was reminded of something our leader, Ray Dalio, said at every other meeting: "You can have anything you want. But you cannot have everything. So you better pick."

I sat in my office on a relatively quiet afternoon and started to map out my strengths. I mapped out my weaknesses. I wrote out my beliefs about myself and my worldview. And I started to come to a conclusion that I felt deeply inside but had not been able to articulate previously. I was climbing the wrong mountain. I was on the wrong trajectory. The mountain I was climbing might be someone else's version of greatness, but it wasn't mine. I was good at it, but it wasn't what fueled my soul -- and if I were to be on my deathbed, and I were to meet the "person I could have become," I would be meeting someone very different.

I was lucky.

I was lucky to be in a company that encouraged this type of self-reflection. I was in a company that offered me the tools necessary to even think about life in this type of abstract and proactive way. Conversely, my immigrant and middle-class upbringing taught a different way of thinking: Be thankful and grateful for what you have. Keep your head down and do the work. Earn your keep and do the best you can.

And yet, on the other hand, here I was in a company that encouraged me to think bigger, to think conceptually, not just in how we operated the business, but in how we operate our lives.

We're not all that lucky. Part of why I wrote this book and even created Unstoppable was so that I can get others to realize that they can all find just 15 minutes on an idle Sunday afternoon to think about their lives in a proactive way. I wanted to provide people with the framework I developed over a decade of the most productive and successful years of my life so more people on this planet can unlock success and achieve their biggest goals. And most importantly, I wanted to get in front of people and INSPIRE them to take 15 minutes to think more proactively about their lives. It worked for me, and it can work for you.

Here's the question, though. Do you want it?

Sitting for even 15 minutes and envisioning what you can become can be a scary thing to do. Because it can deeply challenge your current situation in your life. It can potentially challenge major life decisions you've made in the past. It can make you think about long-held beliefs and force you to rethink whether they are TRUE.

On one hand, doing this type of work, even for 15 minutes, can get you to look reality in the face and really assess where you are. On the other hand, it is SO much easier to just escape and go back to what we're doing: binge-watch Netflix, or open up a beer and hang out with our buddies. That is SO much easier. And I did that for years upon years. Until. Until I said: Enough is enough.

In the subsequent chapters of this book, I'm going to get into the actionable steps you can take in order to start to pause and reflect on your life, and start to really think about what you want. You can have anything, I truly believed that and still do today. But as Ray said: You cannot have everything, so you better pick.

At age 28, nearly two years after I started to really realize that I needed to change the trajectory of my life, I took the plunge. I quit my six-figure job. I got rid of my fancy BMW. And I took the plunge to start my own business again -- something that I felt was core to the trajectory I wanted and needed in my life. Why two years? Because we all have rent, bills, obligations, family, and responsibilities.

When I came to my realization, I took a hard look at reality, and then I said, OK, the trajectory I am on, my status quo, will not get me to the best version of myself and the dream I have for my life. And so I sat down and plotted. I created a vision of who I want to become, and I spent the next two years carefully navigating my life's trajectory closer and closer to the path that I knew would get me to a point where on my deathbed, I'd be looking at myself in the mirror instead of meeting a stranger.

Achieving a proactive life doesn't mean you make crazy rash changes. It also doesn't mean that you succumb to your limitations and surrender, saying, "That's impossible for me." It means that one week at a time, one year at a time, you move your life to align with the vision you have for yourself. At age 28, I started my business. At age 31, I became financially independent. At age 36, I sold my business, then helped sell the business that bought mine, and then moved even closer to the life's path that I had defined for myself at age 25. I did this by focusing full-time on Unstoppable and projects that I deeply cared about. I dreamt. I believed. I executed with Discipline. And I triumphed. Not overnight. Not without setbacks and roadblocks and failures along the way. But little by little, one Unstoppable Sunday at a time.

What does the status quo of your life look like? If you change nothing, if you keep going down your current path, if you do that for decades? What will your life be? When you meet the BEST VERSION OF YOURSELF will you be staring at a mirror image of yourself at your deathbed, or will you be meeting a stranger?

You have a choice to make. As we get into the next few chapters, where I give you the actionable steps to follow, this Unstoppable Life framework, will you do the work or will you have another beer?

Look, I'm not saying that what you're doing right now is wrong. For me, parts of my life BEFORE I made these major changes were great, and parts were off. But I always felt uncertain about my life and I felt a pit in my stomach every Sunday, wondering "Where am I even going?!" Following the steps help you get clarity on where you are, where you are going, and what you need to do next, and help you to take a more proactive approach to life, so that you don't have to wonder.

So what will your choice be? Assess and evaluate the status quo? Or watch Netflix? You pick.

Chapter 3,
Questions to Ask Yourself

Where will you be in ten years if you maintain the status quo?

What are the great things in your life that exist and that you want to maintain, of the status quo?

What are the things you want to change about the status quo?

What are the big macro worldly trends that may put your life at risk?

```
┌─────────────────────────────────────────────┐
│                                             │
│                                             │
│                                             │
│                                             │
│                                             │
│                                             │
│                                             │
└─────────────────────────────────────────────┘
```

Will you be meeting your mirror image or a complete stranger at your deathbed?

    O Complete stranger

    O Mirror image

    O I honestly don't know, but I sure as heck would love to meet my mirror image!

What is the ONE thing you can change today that brings you closer to the best dream version of yourself?

```
┌─────────────────────────────────────────────┐
│                                             │
│                                             │
│                                             │
│                                             │
│                                             │
└─────────────────────────────────────────────┘
```

Chapter 3,
Actions to Take

☐ Building a proactive life for yourself and adopting this framework requires some time every Sunday. Can you commit to even 30 minutes every Sunday to work on this? Will you schedule in time on your calendar to do this?

☐ If you've got a partner, or a family, or even best friends, can you have a conversation with them about how you will commit to spending this time so that you can become a better version of yourself? Would any of them even join you on working on this together?

CHAPTER 4:
EFFECT CHANGE IN YOUR LIFE WITH A 45-DAY CHALLENGE

"Change is hard at first, messy in the middle, and gorgeous at the end."

— Robin S. Sharma

Making changes in life so that you can reap the rewards you want is hard. I'll be honest. Driving the right kind of change takes focus, it takes discipline, it takes commitment. And in this chapter I'm going to give you a tool that you can use as leverage to drive this change. But let's first talk about why you need to make a change and why it is important to commit up front to it.

Congratulations. You've just hit a critical inflection point in this book. Over the past few chapters, we talked through what separates the DREAMERS from the DABBLERS. We talked about our deep-rooted fears and the limiting beliefs holding us back. And, most importantly, we took a moment to pause and imagine what life would be like for you if you maintained the STATUS QUO in an ever-changing world.

If you're continuing to read my book, it means one thing: You're intent on committing to Belief x Discipline and changing the trajectory of your life. I'm pumped for you.

When I was sitting there at age 25, thinking about the trajectory of my life, I knew I had a lot of things to figure out, and I knew I had some changes to make. From age 25 to age 35, I used the same tools that I am going to present to you over the next few chapters of this book. I used these tools to take stock of everything I had accomplished in my life, to craft a vision for my life true to my own definition of greatness, and to then start to navigate toward that vision, one Sunday at a time.

Why Sunday? Because we as human beings love "fresh starts." That is why we love New Year's Resolutions. It is a new beginning and a new opportunity. Similarly, our bodies recognize the fresh start and tighten up on a Sunday. It's a new beginning, and our body is subtly asking us: "What's the plan?"

The subsequent chapters of this book are going to introduce you to actionable ideas that you can adopt in order to bring change to your life. These practices will help you go from just reacting to life to taking control and becoming more proactive in life.

Those changes that I made in my life unlocked nearly a decade of success and productivity for me. The methods, tools, and ideas I used to make those changes came from hundreds of hours of reading, researching, going to conferences, and talking to mentors. Ironically, none of the things that I learned were taught in schools; they weren't taught by my teachers; they weren't taught by my parents; they weren't even taught in the world-class corporations like GE and Bridgewater Associates where I worked. And yet, it is all knowledge that has been available for us to access for thousands of years.

Part of my motivation to write this book was exactly that. I thought it was silly that I wasn't handed a basic, actionable, and simple handbook on how to plan out what I want from life right at the sixth grade. While I was proud of what I had accomplished at age 25, can you imagine just how much farther along I would've been had I learned how to set a vision for my life and how to set goals and how to manage my time and prioritize --- instead of learning how to compute derivatives in Calculus class?!

Before you can start to take action and adopt the mindset that the subsequent chapters of this book will present to you, you'll have to make a decision and make a commitment to **change your status quo and the current trajectory of your life**, so that you can become Unstoppable.

There are certain changes in life that are easy to adopt. It just so happens that they're often not good for us, but we adopt them anyway -- because those easily-adoptable types of changes tend to give us an immediate reward.

On one hand, if you have a drink of Scotch or eat an amazing steak, you almost immediately get the reward and gratification from it, even though in the long term it may be bad for you. Convincing yourself to have steak and Scotch every day is very easy!

On the other hand, if you work out at the gym just once, you feel okay, but it may take 45 days straight of workouts before your body starts to tighten up and you start to feel amazing both physically and mentally. Convincing yourself to go to the gym three times a week in order to reap the long-term rewards can be very hard!

The going-to-the-gym reward is delayed, even though the net positive impact on your life is far greater than is the impact of the Scotch-and-steak meal. But in order to get to that reward, you'll have to make the change in your life to work out for 45 days to reap the long-term, positive rewards of that change. Therein lies the conundrum.

We optimize our lives and build habits that give us immediate gratification, and yet we yearn for the results and success that come from things that require discipline and delayed gratification. In life, whether we realize it or not, we're constantly faced with the choice between discipline now versus regret later.

So the question becomes... How do you start doing the things that provide delayed gratification (thus avoiding that later regret) when doing so means that you are giving up rewards RIGHT NOW? The greatest treasures in life come from delayed gratification and focused and purposeful work through discipline. How do you build Discipline? How do you get unstuck and start taking action on the things that you know are good for you long-term?

You need to start by building momentum. Once you are done working through this book, and once you create the habits to drive change in your life, you will become an Unstoppable freight train.

However, much like any locomotive, you first have to get the momentum going. Which brings me to the key focus of this chapter. How do you get that initial change going? How do you take that first sustainable change? How do you create that Discipline? Especially when you might not feel the rewards right away?

First, the key to getting started is to actually start. This is why I've structured the steps you need to take in this book by prioritizing the things that give you shorter-term rewards. We'll start with practicing Unstoppable Sundays, where you can start to take stock of just the immediate seven days of your life and where you are now, just so you can positively impact the next seven days in your life. Simple, right? Then, as you start to get that momentum, you'll start to think about the next 365 days. And then we'll get to the deeper and meatier aspects of your life plan by starting to look at the next five years of your life, looking at your circles of influence, and looking at taking on bigger challenges that shift the direction of your life.

Second, I've learned over the past decade that there is a distinct art to bringing change into your life. If you start too fast, try to get too big, and move too fast, then you'll fall apart before you even get going. You'll give up. That's why I hate 50% of the lose-weight-fast, change-your-life fast, and become-a-millionaire-easily-tomorrow books. They cause more disillusionment than success because they set expectations too high and people give up before they can reap any rewards; thus, the readers of those books only go back to their old habits. "I tried it... It didn't work. I must not be meant for more." Incorrect. You didn't approach it with a long-term-enough view.

I've learned that in order to bring long-term and sustained success to life, you have to approach change in multiple phases and with a long-term view. You also have to approach it with commitment, discipline, and purposeful and focused action. If what I just said sounds contradictory, well, it might be -- but that is why long-term sustained change is art and not science. It's two opposing and seemingly diverging forces coming together as one.

This is why, as you set out to bring about change, you have to start in the right way. This means that you're not going to feel THAT different tomorrow as you start. Nor will you feel THAT different a week from now. But as you sustain your actions and work at change for a specific period of time, you'll start to build momentum and you'll start to see small rewards. As you work at it for a year, your following year will be even better. Much like the locomotive that starts out slow and sluggish at the station and then picks up speed and becomes Unstoppable, as you continue on your journey toward Unstoppability, you will become Unstoppable, like that locomotive.

So the question is, how do you start? How do you start the RIGHT way? It took me years to master all the core principles around how to do this right. But there is one tool that I now use regularly and that makes it easy for even beginners to start the right way. It's what I call the 45-day Unstoppable Beast Mode Challenge. Let me explain.

A 45-Day Unstoppable Beast Mode Challenge consists of the following:

- **Dream and Establish Belief:** You set a clear intention and goal that you will work to accomplish over the next 45 days.

- **Commitment:** You identify what accomplishing this goal will mean for your life; what it will mean for your life if you DO NOT accomplish it; and then, most importantly, you make a promise to yourself about how you will reward yourself when you do accomplish the goal.
- **Discipline:** You establish a schedule for when you will work on this goal, and you create an action plan for how you will accomplish this goal. You also define the key metrics by which you will measure the progress on your goal.
- **Pause and Reflect:** You will check in every Sunday on how this goal is progressing. You will course-correct your action plan. And you will tweak your approach to ensure success toward your goal.
- **Win and Build Momentum:** At the end of the 45-day period, you will take stock of what you've accomplished, and then you will define your next 45-day Beast Mode Challenge, based on what you've learned from the previous 45 days.

A 45-day Beast Mode Challenge is something I've used countless times in my life when I wanted to start something new, when I wanted to build a new habit that I knew would be good for me, and when I felt like I was stuck on a project and needed to unlock massive productivity.

While it seems simple to say "Just do a 45-day Challenge!" the mechanics of doing a Challenge tap into all the core principles needed to bring change into our lives. Let me walk you through the mechanics of WHY this works.

Dream and Establish Belief

We talked about this in an earlier chapter. In order to bring change and be successful in our lives, we must dream big and establish Belief that what we dream is possible. But so often, dreams can be daunting and Belief can be just a tad bit beyond our reach.

By looking at a 45-day window of time, you allow yourself to ask... "OK... What is a small and meaningful win that I can accomplish within this short period of time?" It also forces you to think... "If I have to worry about just this ONE thing and I wholeheartedly pursue it, could I do it?"

By shrinking the problem space and going after a small step toward a larger goal in your life, by time-boxing it to just 45 days, something magical happens. Belief becomes just a tad bit closer to the span of your reach, just close enough for you to actually grab it.

COMMITMENT

Nothing happens in our lives unless we commit to it. When we commit, we pledge to put in the time toward it, we pledge to overcome the obstacles that stand in our way, and, most importantly, when we commit, we decide to focus on it.

The thing is that commitment doesn't come for free. Commitment comes when we decide that our goal is a MUST instead of a NICE TO HAVE. This is why as part of a 45-day Challenge, we help you visualize and understand what accomplishing this goal would mean to you, how it would change your life. We also have you visualize what it would mean if you DIDN'T do it. How would you be negatively impacted by it? How would you fall behind in your longer-term life goals if you didn't do this one important thing today and over the next 45 days?

By thinking through the repercussions on your life both in the short term and the long term, we help you conceptualize why this goal and this challenge is a MUST DO for your life, and thereby we help you drive commitment to your 45-day Challenge and goal.

DISCIPLINE

Accomplishing and winning in life is EASY. That's right, I said it! The formula for winning is easy. Most of us, the DABBLERS, just don't want to do it. My most favorite saying in the world is: "Discipline now versus Regret later." Discipline is having the sustained routines established that allow us to continuously work toward our goals no matter what.

And so, as part of the 45-day Challenge, we have you open up your calendar and establish work blocks where you will continuously work on your 45-day Challenge. No. Matter. What. That's Discipline. That's Unstoppability. No matter the road blocks, no matter the competing priorities. We commit and establish the Discipline that we MUST work on this challenge and accomplish our goal.

Pause and Reflect

Very rarely in life do things go according to plan. In fact, for every great endeavor that I take on, I expect to hit roadblocks; I expect to learn about flaws in my plan and my approach. And because of these expectations, I always set aside time to pause and reflect.

When we're deep in the thick of things, we get so enamored in the details and knee-deep in the details, that we stop being able to see the forest for the trees. And because I expect this, I explicitly set aside time on Sunday afternoons to NOT DO WORK, and to instead just pause and reflect.

- How are things going?
- What am I doing that is working?
- What am I doing that is NOT working?
- What's stopping me that I need to fix?

We'll talk in greater detail about the practice of Unstoppable Sundays, where we pause and reflect, in a subsequent chapter. But I want you to flag this in your mind right now. As part of your 45-day Challenge, you will set aside time on Sundays to pause and reflect and just that. So that you can course-correct along the way.

You see. Here's the thing. Being UNSTOPPABLE doesn't get you to perfection. It's that you get to a state of mind where, regardless of the roadblocks that you face, you find a way to overcome them and continue toward your goal. Pausing and reflecting helps you do exactly that.

Win and Build Momentum

You are going to accomplish your 45-day goal. I know it. Deep down inside, if you commit, practice Discipline, pause and reflect, and execute, you, too, know that you will.

Have you ever noticed how the rich get richer? How do the winners just keep winning more? There is one simple reason for it: MOMENTUM.

When you get a small win, you go after another win, and then another, and then another, and much like that Unstoppable freight train from hell screeching along the tracks at full speed, you gain so much momentum that you keep winning more and more.

That's why these 45-day Challenges work. Each one allows you to take a small step. A successful Challenge helps you FEEL what winning is like, and then your subsequent Challenges, one after another, start to build more and more momentum and you keep winning.

Throughout the last decade, I've often finished one 45-day Challenge only to kick off another, bigger one. It's an amazing feeling when you win. It is addicting. It is contagious. And these 45-day Challenges help you get unstuck from the patterns in your life that stop you from winning and help you build momentum to create one win after another.

Can you imagine where you'll be five years fro now, if you practice Belief x Discipline? I've done it for the past decade and this practice has brought me great fortune, great success, and, most importantly, fulfillment and the ability and freedom and wealth to do whatever I want and to effect the change I want to see in this world.

The Next 45 Days of Your Life

Starting with the next chapter, I'm going to begin teaching you the core tools I have used over the past decade, and continue to use today, to live an Unstoppable and proactive life.

These tools will help you realize the promise of this book: to live a proactive life and go GET the life that you deserve. The life that your family deserves. The life that your loved ones deserve. So that at your deathbed, you are not meeting a complete stranger, but you are meeting a mirror image of you, the absolute BEST VERSION of you.

Here's the thing, though: You will not succeed in adopting these tools, you will not succeed in adopting these new habits, and you will not succeed in changing the trajectory of your life, if you do not commit.

How do you commit?

We'll kick off a 45-day Challenge, of course.

I want you to kick off a 45-day Challenge starting today -- to adopt the ideas I am going to present to you in the subsequent chapters of this book.

I want you to kick off a 45-day Challenge starting today -- to commit to making a change in your life.

I want you to kick off a 45-day Challenge in which you will schedule in time to WORK on this.

I want you to kick off a 45-day Challenge in which you will spend every Sunday afternoon to pause and reflect by practicing Unstoppable Sundays.

I want you to kick off a 45-day Challenge in which you will map out your next seven days, then your next 365 days, and then your five-year vision for your life.

Over the next 45 days, you will turn this book -- which has just my words and empty boxes -- into a concrete, proactive plan for your life. This book will become your book. Your roadmap. Your path to the life that you deserve.

Are you ready?

Chapter 4,
Questions to Ask Yourself

Are you willing to commit to a 45-day Challenge to create a life plan for yourself?
O Yes
O No, I'm good with the status quo, give me my money back

What is my ONE measurable 45-day goal?

To wholeheartedly adopt the tools presented in the subsequent chapters in this book.

At the end of this 45-day Challenge, I will have:

- Practiced Unstoppable Sundays every Sunday to pause and reflect.

- Created a 365-day proactive life plan for myself.

- Created a 365-day proactive life calendar for myself.

- Created a five-year vision for myself.

- Created a support network of like-minded and growth-oriented people around me who will support me in my life goal and plan.

What would life look like after I've accomplished my 45-day goal?

What will happen to my life if I do not do this now?

What does the status quo of my life look like?

How would I dramatically move forward my agenda in my life if I succeed?

How will I celebrate and reward myself when I accomplish this goal?

What will successfully completing this challenge mean for my loved ones?

What bigger things can I pursue after I lock in this WIN and build MOMENTUM in my life?

Who else can I convince to do this 45-day Challenge along with me? (optional)

Chapter 4,
Actions to Take

☐ Open up your calendar and let's schedule in time for you to work on this 45-day Challenge. Here are the things you need to schedule in:

- Every Sunday afternoon, "Practice Unstoppable Sundays" for 30 minutes.
- At least twice a week, instead of watching Netflix, "Work on my Unstoppable Life Plan" for an hour and a half.
- At least once a week, instead of going out every night, "Work on my action plans on my 365-day goals." (Don't worry. In a later chapter, we'll walk you through clarifying your goals. But let's schedule in the time right now to work explicitly on these goals.)

☐ Grab your phone. Take a picture of your commitment to this 45-day Challenge from the worksheet you just completed. Make it your wallpaper or set it as a favorite picture so that you can often go back to this picture and remind yourself of the commitment you just made.

☐ One last thing: You might be an overachiever (like I am) and you may be able to create your life plan, and to complete this book and the worksheets well before the 45-day deadline. There is NO SPEED LIMIT to life. If you finish ahead of time, you can always declare victory early and kick off a NEW 45-day Unstoppable Beast Mode Challenge centered around one or more of your 365-day goals. Consider this a challenge. ;)

☐ Onwards

CHAPTER 5:

GET RID OF THE SUNDAY SCARIES: PRACTICE UNSTOPPABLE SUNDAYS

"A Sunday well spent brings a week of content."

— Proverb

We've all been there. It's Sunday, and that feeling deep down in our gut starts to creep in. It's the pre-Monday, "Oh-God-why-isn't-this-a-four-day-weekend?" dreary feeling. It's the "What am I even doing with my life?" feeling. It's the "I love my job. I love my job. I love my job... If I keep saying it, it'll come true..." feeling. It's the feeling that lingers through Monday and into Wednesday, as you count down to the weekend, feeling -- and it's the "hamster-wheel-of-life" feeling, because you've been on it for nearly a decade and you're not quite sure whether it's worth it all.

Where am I even going?

At 27, I felt like I had it all. As an immigrant kid from Bangladesh who had spent the first ten years of his life there, then moved to grow up in Flushing, Queens in a one-bedroom apartment where six people lived together -- now, my townhouse, my sports car with the red leather seats, my double degree in Computer Science and Management from a prestigious institution, my office -- all of it showed that I had MADE IT. And yet, I dreaded every Monday. I was deep in my finance job at one of the most successful hedge funds in the world and I experienced that feeling. I kept asking myself --- there's supposed to be a K'ABoom! Where's the K'ABoom?!

I knew I couldn't make dramatic changes on a whim -- I had far too much to lose and I didn't exactly have a trust fund to fall back on. So, I started to take it a day at a time to start to figure out: Where am I?... and What do I do next?

Between the years 2010 and 2018, I started to set aside 30 minutes every Sunday to answer those two simple questions. Much as you might spend your Sunday doing chores to keep your house running and in order, I started to spend a portion of every Sunday thinking about and writing down where I am and what I wanted next out of my life.

For some reason, when I first started to practice this simple exercise, it just made me feel better. It instantly helped me stop feeling restless and I immediately started to feel like I was in the driver's seat for a change.

Through that nine-year period, the simple exercise of pausing and reflecting unlocked unparalleled productivity and growth for me as a person. I went from being a Product Manager at a hedge fund to quitting my job to starting my own company. I went on to scale my company from 0 to 70 people and went from $0 in revenue to millions in annual recurring revenue. I went from being CEO of that successful venture to selling it to a market leader and joining their executive team as the youngest Senior Vice President in the company's history. It doesn't stop there: We then went on to sell that company to one of the largest technology companies in the world.

Throughout that ten-year period, I went from living paycheck-to-paycheck to being financially independent. Throughout that ten-year period, I went from being reactive to my life and just doing what was expected of me, to taking control of a vision for my life and executing on it.

As Step 1 of this Unstoppable Life system, I want you to start practicing this simple exercise, because it will be your first step in assessing your current situation and starting to become more proactive about your life, just one week at a time.

Most importantly, this will be your first step in eradicating the Sunday Scaries, the Sunday angst, the Sunday "What am I even doing with my life?!" existential crisis.

This ten-year period of productivity and success resulted in large part from this simple exercise I call Unstoppable Sundays. Every Sunday, I sit down, I open up my document (which is now 200+ pages), and I **answer the two questions: Where am I? And... What do I do next?**

The most important thing to do is to start carving out just 30 minutes every Sunday, and start to take your time reflecting on these two questions and recording the answers in this document.

Because I've been using the same document over the years, I'm able to scroll back years at a time to review how I was feeling and what I was tackling on any given Sunday. Because I write down my thoughts, I'm able to really think through and conceptualize my deepest subconscious feelings.

Your ability to write well, your ability to write something that may sound wrong, or your likelihood to "get it wrong" -- NONE of these things matters. This document is for you, by you, and so you have to treat it as an extension of your inner thoughts. All this does is to get your thoughts out of your head and onto paper, which then allows you to take a step back and really understand what is going on.

I also like starting with a seven-day view, because so many personal development books tell you to think big, dream big, and you'll accomplish it all. That's just plain unrealistic. I get it; I've been there. There are existing commitments, real constraints, bills to pay, and things to finish. So, I always like to prompt you to start by reflecting on where you are and getting your week in order. Over time, you can start to get even more proactive about your next month, then your next year. And as you start to appreciate how you will operate within your current situation just that much better, we can start to think bigger and figure out what walls to knock down to remodel the house and make it your dream house (and life)!

It's important not to overcomplicate this. All you need to do is open up a Word document on a Sunday, write down the date, and start to answer these two questions. Easy! And from my experience and what I've heard from our community practicing Unstoppable Sundays, you'll quickly start to feel at ease about the week ahead instead of trying to escape from the Sunday Scaries.

The simple practice of doing this every Sunday does a few things for me. First, it eliminates my Sunday anxieties. It provides an immediate outlet for all the feelings that might otherwise rush through my head about Monday. Second, it allows me to stay tethered to a stream of consciousness. I am easily able to look back at where I was last Sunday and what I had committed to doing and how I was feeling, and thus I'm able to compare to see whether this Sunday I'm doing better or worse. And, third, it allows me to be proactive about my situation instead of trying to escape it; I do this by laying out an action plan for the next seven days.

These two questions of Where am I? and What do I do next? are seemingly simple. Here's how to think about answering them and why they are just so powerful.

WHERE AM I?

This question is designed to help you take stock of where you are right now in your life.

- How would I describe my current situation?
- What am I feeling? Anger? Frustration? Happiness? Anxiousness? Worry?
- What are my current sources of anxiety? What am I worried about?

- What's going on in my inner monologue? You know... that pesky voice inside our heads...

Not only is it incredibly cathartic to get it all out of my head and onto paper, but this process of writing and articulating what is going on in my head and my subconscious also allows me to gain a deeper understanding around exactly what I am feeling, and it'll do the same for you.

WHAT DO I DO NEXT?

- One of the core principles of Unstoppable is purposeful and focused ACTION. Raise hell and be badass, I say. Go punch that obstacle in the face! reads my iPhone wallpaper.
- If all I did on Sundays was spend 30 minutes pontificating about my thoughts, I would not have experienced the decade of productivity that I just did.
- In this part of the exercise, I look at "Where I am..." and then create a bulleted list of the action steps I need to take in the coming week in order to start moving forward in terms of my goals for the year.
- Mind you, this isn't meant to be a to-do list; you keep that elsewhere. THIS is more of your inner voice syncing with YOU on... "All right... Given everything that is going on, here's what I'm going to do to move forward."
- I capture these items in bullet points, a few paragraphs, and, honestly, it varies from long ramblings to succinct bullet points. It doesn't matter how you capture it; what does matter is that you take the time to pause and reflect on where you are and then to define/refine and write down your action plan to move forward.
- Note that your action plan may not vary wildly from week to week. That's OK. Sometimes, I'll look at my action plan from the prior week and just copy-paste the same. Sometimes, I'll realize that last

week's plan just doesn't make sense, or that it isn't realistic, and I'll chart a new approach. Either way, what matters is that you do have a plan, that you are proactive, and that you write down your plan and commit to it so that you can keep yourself honest.

To make it even easier for you to begin the practice of Unstoppable Sundays, we've created a web-based application and online community for everyone reading this book and practicing Unstoppable Sunday to become a high performing person and living a proactive life. Just go to: https://getunstoppable.com/life.

Something magical will begin to happen as you start to practice Unstoppable Sundays. First, you'll find that you're going into each week with a plan. That alone should put your mind at ease as you execute on your week. But, more importantly, as you start the ball rolling on Unstoppable Sundays, and as this becomes a habit week after week, you'll start to ask yourself: Well…. Here's where I am… Here's what I'm going to do in the coming week… But where am I going?

The first hurdle to overcome as you create a life strategy and plan you can tether yourself to, is to establish the practice of pausing and reflecting on a weekly basis. In the next chapter, we'll help you think through how to start reflecting on your life through a broader, 365-day aperture, so that you can tether these weekly sessions to a broader plan for your life.

Lastly, do remember that you're not in this alone. There's a whole community of people who practice Unstoppable Sundays.

If you learn something new every Sunday (from our community) and spend 30 minutes every Sunday to become proactive about your life -- can you even begin to imagine what you're going to accomplish over the coming decade? Onwards!

Now here's the thing: You can just read this book, make a bunch of mental notes, and just move on with your life. That is not going to be what brings about transformative change in your life. The only way you will change the trajectory of your life and get to a proactive lifestyle is if you actually start practicing now. So for this chapter and onwards, there will be a worksheet for you to follow right now as you read so that you can start taking focused and purposeful action right now in changing your life.

Let's start making a change in your life right now. Let's practice Unstoppable Sundays together, right now.

Chapter 5,
Questions to Ask Yourself

How do you typically feel on a Sunday afternoon as you start to think about Monday and the week ahead?

What are the things you typically "escape" to so that you do not have to think about the week ahead? What do you do to ignore or "feel better but not solve" the angst and the pit in your stomach on a Sunday afternoon or evening?

What are the non-negotiable commitments that you have on a Sunday afternoon that you must do and cannot get out of? These are okay to have, let's just acknowledge those things here.

When on a Sunday could you schedule in 15 to 30 minutes on your calendar, or an alarm on your phone, so that you are reminded to pause and reflect?

What small "escapism" on a Sunday could you delay or give up so that you can start to get proactive about your life and your coming week?

Let's try our first Unstoppable Sunday (even if right NOW is not a Sunday) together. Just to see how it feels and get you going.

Where am I?

What do I do next?

Chapter 5,
Actions to Take

☐ Schedule a time into your calendar or set an alarm on your phone for every Sunday for your 15 to 30 minutes of Pausing and Reflection time; for practicing Unstoppable Sundays.

☐ Pick a spot where you can have some peace and quiet so you can practice Unstoppable Sundays.

☐ Subscribe to our Web-Based Unstoppable Sunday application and online community: https://www.getunstoppable.com/life

☐ Practice your first Unstoppable Sunday in this book and then start practicing it every Sunday using the web-based application.

☐ Onwards!

CHAPTER 6:

GET PROACTIVE ABOUT THE NEXT 365 DAYS OF YOUR LIFE

"Tomorrow, is the first blank page of a 365 page book. Write a good one."

— Brad Paisley

In order to be successful in life, you need an Unstoppable strategy, and a plan to implement that strategy through purposeful and focused ACTION.

Strategy can be a complicated word; it can even seem fru-fru when you think of it in the context of your own life. But it doesn't have to be. In fact, it shouldn't be.

Great strategy is the efficient organization of resources. Your resources. Your most precious resources, such as your time, your money, your conscious attention, and, most importantly, the inner monologue of your mind.

When you think of strategy in simple terms like that, all of a sudden it sounds absolutely crazy that so many of us go through life without having thought through a strategy (an efficient organization of our resources) that we can tether ourselves to and improve over time as we learn.

For all of us, regardless of how much money we have in the bank, the most scarce resource we have is time. How you spend your time, what you burn your calories on in a given 24-hour period, is the most critical strategic decision you have to make in your life. And, yet, we spend our days working at jobs we don't love; we spend our evenings cruising Netflix to de-stress from the perils of the day; and we spend our weekends getting drunk with people who won't help us grow, but who will help us pass our time so we can go back to Monday and count down to the next weekend -- only to do it all over again. I call this the Hamster Wheel of Life.

As you start to move into the discipline of practicing Unstoppable Sundays, as you start to hone in on "Where am I" and "What do I do next" -- something magical will happen. You'll stop reacting to every day of your life and you'll start to be proactive about how you take on each day. And as you shift your consciousness from being reactive to being proactive, from having a fixed mindset to having a growth mindset, you'll naturally start to ask yourself some seriously strategic questions about your life: What's the big plan? What do I want to accomplish over the next 12 months of my life? Where do I want to be five years from now?

Now that I've shown you how to become proactive about the next seven days of your life, it's time to start zooming out a bit and thinking about the next 365 days of your life and time to start laying out a strategy and plan: Think of this as if you were plotting a bank heist.

Before I show you the Unstoppable way of planning the next 356 days of your life, let's just talk through the BEFORE of how I used to try to plan life, and how most people still do that today.

BEFORE I developed this system, I didn't think of yearly planning as an active sport. It was a passive activity that happened unofficially between Christmas and New Year's. Nothing was written down; there was no reviewing of last year's goal; it was all in my head during brief moments of time.

BEFORE I developed this system, my goals really consisted of a wish list of common New Year's Resolutions around losing weight, making more money, and finally quitting my job to start that dream business. I also really wanted to learn another language... Yeah, that'd be great, too.

BEFORE I developed this system, even if I set some resolutions or goals, I'd pretty quickly forget about them -- or, even worse, become uninspired by them and kind of just go back to the grind by the time February rolled around. In fact, 80 percent of people break their New Year's Resolutions by the time the second week of February arrives. Sound familiar?

Truth is, you can go to the most prestigious schools and universities, yet never will you actually find a class on how to create a strategy and plan for your life.

This whole system of goal-setting is flawed due to three reasons:

1. First, we completely overestimate how much we can actually accomplish in the 365 days of the year. First, 365 days, or a year, feels like a long time. But when you really break it down, out of the 365 days, there are only 261 working days, and after you take away vacation days, you're down to 247 working days, and after you subtract sick days, down time, and family commitments, you're left with a mere 220 days, or roughly seven-and-a-half months out of every year to really take action on your goals.

2. Second, we don't set up a system to be proactive about our yearly goals as we work through the year. So, we become uninspired about our goals, we forget them, and we return to just reacting to the day-to-day. Finally, the next year rolls around, and we ask ourselves: "Where did the time go?!" only to adopt the same defunct goals all over again -- sound familiar?

3. Last, while we may fail at achieving the goals that we overestimated our ability to accomplish, we also, at the same time, fail to

acknowledge and give gratitude for whatever DID go well during the past 365 days, whatever DID work out, that DID move us maybe 20 percent closer to meeting a greater challenge, even if we're not 100 percent there, as we had hoped or anticipated.

Now, let's talk about the AFTER. The Unstoppable Proactive Life Planning system didn't come together all at once for me. It is based on all sorts of different tools that I learned from friends, read about, and developed over the course of a decade. These all came together to unlock a period of unparalleled productivity for me. This system is all rooted in the idea of proactively planning for my life instead of just reacting to it.

AFTER I started to treat my planning process as an active sport, I started to take my goals a lot more seriously.

AFTER I started to check in on my goals on a regular basis, and to pause and reflect on a weekly basis on how I'm doing, I started to execute on my goals a lot more aggressively.

AFTER I started to express gratitude for even the small wins, I started to accomplish greater challenges that took multiple years to execute on -- but I didn't give up along the way.

So for this next step in developing your Unstoppable Proactive Life Plan, we're going to walk you through creating the first version of your strategy and plan for the next 365 days. Why the first version? Because, remember: Kaizen, combining the collective resources at your disposal (your time, your energy, your intellect, your mentors, your friends) to create a powerful engine for improvement in your own life.

This yearly planning process is similar to Unstoppable Sundays, where you answer two questions in a Word document; you'll do the same for this part of the process in a Word document, except that there will be a few more questions.

These very simple questions, to which you will write the answers, will help you pause and reflect about the past 365 days, and then to start to organize around the next 365 days. By taking an hour (or more) to do this, you will accomplish the following:

- Instead of haphazardly setting the same New Year's Resolutions over and over, you will have actively thought through what you want to accomplish over the coming year.
- By answering a couple of simple questions about how your past year went, you will have an opportunity to learn from what went well and what didn't go well over the past year.
- By writing down your goals in a structured way, you will make it easier for yourself to refer back to these goals throughout the course of the year, and then, most importantly, to see, a year from now, how they turned out.

You know what's the best feeling? My favorite, most absolutely, BEST feeling is when I'm at the end of the year, and I'm looking at the list of goals I wrote down at the beginning of the year, and I am able to cross them off one at a time -- because I crushed them! I want you to enjoy that feeling. I want you to experience that feeling of success, of triumph, of winning. So let's get started...

To start, you'll first answer a set of questions that helps you to reflect and learn from the prior year:
1. What are the things I am grateful for?
2. What are the things I am stressed about?
3. What are my key accomplishments over the past year?
4. Looking back, what did I say I would accomplish in the past year? How did this go?
5. Looking back, what is the ONE weakness of mine that held me back the most during the past year?

Again, just as with the Unstoppable Sundays exercise, don't overthink it. All that is important is that you put your thoughts on paper (or screen), so that they're not just percolating in your head.

Once you've gone through the first set of questions, here's how you will be feeling:

- You'll have a renewed sense of the events and circumstances that happened during the past year and that you are thankful for. Our memories are incredibly flawed, and we often have recency bias. Thinking back through the past year and identifying ALL the lucky breaks that went my way and for which I am grateful really helps me hone in on the happenstances that are going well.

- You'll take account of the things that are stressors in your life right now, both in the conscious and the subconscious mind. Dig deep here. Think about the things that are stressing you out and be specific about it all, out on paper. I find this to be incredibly cathartic, and it also helps me start to frame some of the smaller goals I want for the year to address the things in my life that are stressing me out and stopping me from accomplishing bigger things. Even during my BEST years, when I have absolutely crushed it, there were still circumstances, needs, disappointments, personalities, and so on that stressed me out. It's okay. It's life. Describe it all on paper (or screen).

- You'll come away with a succinct list of what you have accomplished during the past year, regardless of what your original goals were. Life throws all kinds of twists and turns, fraught with problems and opportunities. That's normal. And answering the question about your key accomplishments (regardless of what your goals were) again helps you hone in on what went well.

- You'll also go back to the set of goals that you set for yourself a year ago, and you'll check in on how they went. If this is your first time at this and you hadn't set goals a year ago, that's okay -- but just imagine how awesome it's going to be once you write down your goals now, check in on them throughout the year, and then check them all off as "accomplished" at the end of the year!

- And, finally, as you reflect on your wins, your losses, and your stressors, you'll dig deep inside and identify the ONE BIG WEAKNESS that has held you back over the past year. Everyone has one: What's yours? Find it.

After this first set of questions, your mind will probably be racing. You will probably feel invigorated, and you'll feel excited by the prospects that lie ahead in the next 365 days. You might also feel a bit of angst about how you'll ever achieve the objectives you want to in the coming year, given your natural stressors or the circumstances in your life!

Good or bad, excited or scared, the important thing is that you're taking time now to create a plan, instead of relying on hope as your life strategy. Even for the problems that exist in your life, no matter how bad they are, solutions do exist. And know that problems can be opportunities for growth in your life.

Now, as the next-to-last step, you'll start to write down your FIVE key goals for the next 365 days. You've got 365 days ahead of you. How do you want to go and pull off those 365 days like a bank heist, and what treasures would you like in the end? How do you want to overcome your stressors and the problems in your life?

You'll want to answer and capture these questions by writing a set of FIVE clear and easy-to-measure goals. Why five? Because for some reason, anything more just becomes unmanageable. Why measurable? Because a year from now, when you're looking back at these goals, you must be able to answer, without a doubt, whether or not you succeeded in hitting your goals.

You may also want to capture five goals across specific aspects of your life. I usually break these down into core categories. Here are some specific and measurable goals you can set, spanning across the key categories of your life:

1. **Health:** Weight ___ lbs.
2. **Wealth:** Earn $____ after taxes.
3. **Relationships:** Make five new friends that I'm on a texting basis with, who are growth-oriented.
4. **Giving Back:** Spend 14 days of the year volunteering my time to give back to my community or extended family.
5. **Self-Improvement:** Read one book every month.

Given where you are in your life and what your priorities are, these key aspects of your life may vary. Honestly speaking, there were years when I was working on coming out of debt and I just didn't have the ability to prioritize giving back. That's okay. We're all on our own journeys. What is important is that you clearly define what works best for you as you plan where you want to go in life.

Finally, even the world's best strategies are useless unless you follow up with purposeful and focused action. As the final step, I want you to make a bulleted list of the action plan that will help you mobilize these goals.

Use our template to work through this easily: To make it even easier to begin the practice of your 365-day strategy and plan, we've created a simple template that you can use to get started quickly: https://www.getunstoppable.com/templates/365-day-goals

Even if you're spending just one hour to proactively reflect on your past year and to write down specific goals for your coming year, you'll be significantly ahead of the average person out there. By reviewing these goals on a monthly basis, you'll have significantly increased your chances of success.

This process can be daunting. I'm ten years into following this (as the system has evolved over time), and even I can feel overwhelmed at times. Take your time and remember: There is no perfect answer, and you can always tweak the plan as you learn more throughout the year. What matters the most is that you're taking the steps now to craft a strategy, tether yourself to it, and become proactive about your life.

Now remember! This book is not meant to be a piece of art that sits on your bookshelf or one that just gets forgotten. So grab a pen, and let's work through what you've processed through this chapter.

Chapter 6,
Questions to Ask Yourself

Do you typically set New Year's Resolutions? Do you write down goals for yourself every year? What usually happens to them?

How often do you review and check in on your goals throughout the course of a year? If you did it more regularly, would you have been more likely to pursue the right goals and crush them?

What would happen if you sat down, wrote down your goals, and checked in on them every three months to course-correct?

Chapter 6,
Actions to Take

☐ Schedule a time into your calendar or set an alarm on your phone for every 45 days to write down, review, and iterate on your goals.

☐ Pick a spot where you can have some peace and quiet so you can practice goal setting for your life.

☐ Download our 365-day goal setting template, set it up, and start to commit to creating a 365-day proactive plan for yourself: https://www.getunstoppable.com/templates/365-day-goals

☐ Onwards!

Chapter 6,
Bonus Materials

- Watch my episode on How to Go from Having a Fixed Mindset to Having a Growth Mindset, https://www.getunstoppable.com/3-ways-to-invest-in-yourself/
- Watch my episode on Getting Off the Hamster Wheel of Life, https://www.getunstoppable.com/the-hamster-wheel-of-life/
- Watch my episode on How to Be Proactive in Life by Creating a Life Plan, https://www.getunstoppable.com/how-to-be-proactive-in-life/

CHAPTER 7:

GET PROACTIVE ABOUT HOW YOU ALLOCATE YOUR TIME OVER THE NEXT 365 DAYS

There's a famous saying: "

Show me your calendar, and I'll show you your priorities."

Now that you've gotten into the practice of Unstoppable Sundays, and have started to think through your attack strategy for the next 365 days, there's ONE EVIL THING IN YOUR LIFE that you've got to eradicate – and that's your calendar as it stands right now.

Whether we realize it or not, much of our lives is spent according to priorities set by others, who decide what they want us to be doing. Whether it is meetings at work, family commitments on weekends, or those work trips that we're endlessly on – we spend all those hours and days constantly REACTING.

Regardless of what we put on our to-do lists, despite our New Year's Resolutions, and notwithstanding the intentions we set at the beginning of the day -- ultimately it is what is on our calendars that dictates how we spend our time.

So the question then becomes: What is on your calendar? Who is setting the agenda for how you set your time on your calendar? And, if you haven't spent 30 minutes each week to map out the week ahead, and at least a couple hours to map out your next 365 days, do you think you're making the most of your time ahead?

Let me ask you another set of questions. Where will you be spending Thanksgiving? Fourth of July? Christmas? Do you have your two weeks of vacation planned out through the year? How about Spring Break? Have you thought about strategically taking a few long weekends throughout the course of the year to pause, restore yourself, and make sure you're on the right track?

In the BEFORE part of my life, I didn't use my calendar as a proactive tool. And I wouldn't have been able to answer most of the questions I posed above. I was working hard, but not working smart. I was burning through the hours, but only to burn myself out. And worst of all, as the major holidays approached, anticipation of these dates only increased my anxiety level, because I didn't think to properly plan ahead and make the most of them.

In the AFTER part of my life, I became more purposeful about the goals I wanted to accomplish for the year; I started to pause and reflect on a weekly basis. But, most importantly, I began to set up my calendar to cater to my goals instead of others' goals. In the AFTER part of my life, I started to answer these strategic questions about my life and developed the habit of mapping it out ahead of time for the next 365 days:

1. Where, with whom, and how will I spend the major holidays? Here in the United States, these holidays include Memorial Day, Independence Day, Labor Day, Columbus Day, Thanksgiving Day, Christmas, and New Year's.

2. When will I be taking my one major vacation (even if it is a staycation) of the year? Where will I go? Whom will I spend it with?

3. How can I take time away every six to eight weeks, either because of a holiday or as a day off, so that I can pause, reflect, and course-correct on my plan for the year?

4. What are the necessities of life I need to take care of every four to six weeks to ensure I'm running in peak condition? Doctors' appointments? Haircuts? Massage?

5. What major conferences, networking events, and charity functions will I be attending throughout the next 365 days to broaden my network and increase my net worth?

6. What family-and-friends commitments do I have over the next 365 days? These include weddings, birthdays, reunions, etc. Will I prioritize them or decline with regret, based on my other priorities for the year?

7. Given what I've prioritized over the next 365 days, as well as my time commitments, will I be able to accomplish the goals I've set for myself?

You may first notice, as you read the set of questions above, that they're not your average "Do I go to my Monday morning team meeting?" type of calendar questions. These are broader, more strategic questions to answer about how you will spend the next 365 days of your life. These are questions that are designed such that, if you spend 30 to 60 minutes addressing them up front, in a proactive way, your answers will not only help you run the rest of your year smoothly, but your responses will also help you to be proactive and to prioritize the right things in your life.

You'll also notice that most calendar applications (like Microsoft Outlook or iCalendar on the Mac) aren't really designed to map out your year in this way. In fact, most calendar applications are designed for the exact opposite purpose: They're there for others to easily send you calendar invitations to events THEY think are important and to fill up your days.

So, to help you map out and become proactive about the next 365 days of your life, we've created a spreadsheet that helps you map out your whole year. This spreadsheet gives you a MACRO view of your 365 days, instead of being zoomed in to just this week -- or, even worse, just today – which is how we often approach our calendars.

Using this spreadsheet, you'll be able to take a step back and ask yourself some important questions:

1. How many days of the next 365 are already committed? (hint: More than you think.)

2. How many of those commitments are actually important?

3. How many days have I set aside and committed to accomplishing my life goals?

4. How do I plan out the next 8, 12, even 24 weeks of my life so that I know to prioritize and be PROACTIVE about the most important things?

Once you've completed this exercise, you'll have realized and sorted through a few key things:

1. First, 365 days, or a year, feels like a long time. But when you really break it down, out of the 365 days, there are only 261 working days when you can actively work toward your goals both personal and professional. When you take away vacation days, you're down to 247 working days. And when you subtract sick days, down time, and family commitments, you're left with a mere 220 days, or roughly seven-and-a-half months out of every year to really take action on your goals.

2. Second, when we don't take a proactive approach to the 365 days, many decisions are made for us. We find ourselves signed up for a ton of commitments that take away even more of those 220 golden working days. It's no wonder we ask ourselves after a year of not hitting our goals: "Where did all the time go?!" Truth is there wasn't a lot of time to begin with, and after that, others took the remaining time away from us, to be spent on activities that weren't necessarily aligned to our own goals.

3. Most importantly, you'll start to feel a sense of calm and control from having been able to hit head-on some of the tough questions about how you want to spend your year. I always share this spreadsheet with my loved ones so that we can have a discussion about how we want to collectively take on the year. Negotiations on "which parent's house" we need to spend Thanksgiving in become easier; having vacations planned ahead of time gives us something to count down to as we're grinding through the days to work on our goals; and, most importantly, we're able to keep ourselves honest regarding whether we are taking on and prioritizing the right goals for the year.

I open up my 365-day proactive calendar every week during Unstoppable Sundays, to review what's ahead and course-correct as I learn more. Most importantly, it always gives my family and me a sense of calm, because there is a real plan that everyone can rally around and look forward to. No one ever freaks out when there is a plan in place!

Now remember what we said about this book! This book is not meant to be a piece of art that sits on your bookshelf or one that just gets forgotten. So grab a pen, and let's work through what you've processed through this chapter.

Chapter 7,
Questions to Ask Yourself

Have you taken stock of all the time commitments you have through the course of the year? Where will you spend Thanksgiving? Long weekends? Are there critical trips that you have for this year that you still need to plan and account for?

If you could, what are the three key things you'd proactively schedule for yourself throughout the course of the year? Vacations? Long Weekends? A half-day to check in on your goals? A girls' or guys' trip?

What would happen if you mapped out your time commitments and also time for yourself ahead of time in a proactive way instead of having to tend to it last minute?

Chapter 7,
Actions to Take

☐ Make a list of all of your big time commitments for the next 365 days.

☐ Make a list of the trips, activities, and time you'd like to schedule FOR YOURSELF for the next 365 days.

☐ Download our 365-day calendar template, set it up, and start to commit to creating a proactive 365-day schedule for yourself: https://www.getunstoppable.com/templates/365-day-calendar

☐ Onwards!

Chapter 7,
Bonus Materials

- Watch my episode on How to Avoid Burnout, https://www.getunstoppable.com/burnout
- Watch my episode on My New Years Resolution and Goals for 2019, https://www.getunstoppable.com/my-new-years-resolutions-for-2019/

CHAPTER 8:

GET A CLEAR AND PROACTIVE VISION OF "YOU" FIVE YEARS FROM NOW

"Most people overestimate what they can do in one year and underestimate what they can do in ten years."

— Bill Gates

agree. This is why it is super important that you start to take a longer view on life and what you want to accomplish. But before we get into that, let's just take a moment and recognize how far we've come in your journey toward thinking about living a more proactive life.

- **In Chapter 5,** we introduced you to the idea of practicing Unstoppable Sundays, as we taught you to reflect on and plan for your upcoming seven days.
- **In Chapter 6,** we helped you zoom out and start to think about your one-year plan by answering a set of very pointed questions that help you practice gratitude, assess where you are today, and then start to lay out a plan for the next 365 days.

- **In Chapter 7,** we introduced a new tool that you can use to become proactive about the 365 days you're given every year, so that you can be proactive about how you spend your days and months in a given year and can make tough trade-offs on what you spend your time on versus not.

Listen, before I set out to write this book, and before I set out to create an online course on living a more proactive life, I first became aware of the statistics:

- Only 15 percent of people who purchase a course or book about making a change in their lives actually complete it.

- 92 percent of people who set goals never actually achieve them, according to a research study conducted at the University of Scranton.

The reality is that the world has a lot more DABBLERS than DO-ERs. A very small percentage of the population is actually ambitious. The reality is that all the statistics show that you'll have downloaded this book, will have read parts of it, and yet you won't make a single change in your life.

Nevertheless, here are some statistics that are even more daunting, and the reason why I still thought it was worth a shot to write this book and inspire at least 1,000 people to be more proactive in their lives:

- 40 million people today are suffering from anxiety,
- 14.8 million people are suffering from depression,
- and 7.7 million people are suffering from post-traumatic stress disorder.
- In 2016 alone, the U.S. spent 446 billion dollars on medications -- almost half of the global market.

The reality is that people are hurting: They're feeling anxiety and depression, and they're struggling to find true meaning in their lives. And yet they struggle to take the decisive action necessary to break free. More than half of the battle, I believe, is that people aren't given a practical framework for taking action and making changes in their lives. (That is where this book comes in.) And the other half of the battle is that your friends and your family won't let you. (More on this in the next chapter.)

Why say all of this now? Well, if you've reached this chapter, or if you've skimmed this far ahead, that means you've got a chance. You've got a chance to be one of the select few on this planet who can break free, take decisive action, and make necessary and critical changes in your life.

And so that's why I'm here checking in with you. Have you started to practice Unstoppable Sundays? Have you started to think about the next seven days? Have you answered some of the tough questions about what you've accomplished, and started to lay out goals for the next 365 days?

It's easy to read a book. It's easy to dabble. It's harder to actually DO what's necessary to make the changes and go punch your goals in the face.

But you know what's harder? Lack. Not having enough. Or even worse, poverty.

You know what's harder? Regret.

You know what's even harder? Not being able to live the life that you know you deserve.

All of those things are harder. Much harder, than actually facing your reality and taking essential action to go chase down your goals.

You now have a choice to make. You have to choose between being a DABBLER and a DO-er. Will you just continue skimming through this book? Or are you going to begin work? Are you going to start taking the steps that will change your life?

The next step in your journey of becoming Unstoppable is to develop a longer view of your life. When it comes to developing a long-term, proactive view of your life, you must look at life through three lenses (zoom levels, as I like to refer to them):

- How am I going to proactively spend the next week of my life? This is what Unstoppable Sundays are all about (Chapter 5).
- How am I going to spend the next 365 days of my life? I go through a very specific yearly planning process to define this (Chapters 6 and 7).
- And, finally: What do I want my life to look like five years from now? This is your macro view. This one is super-important, because we tend to OVERESTIMATE what we can accomplish in a year, and we tend to grossly UNDERESTIMATE what we can accomplish in five to ten years.

There's a trick here. We first have you grab hold of your current situation by looking at seven days, and then at 365 days. Then, we'll have you start to think about the next five years. The longer view helps you break out of the current constraints in your life and start to think about the necessary transformations you can bring over the next half-decade to full decade. As you think through this, you'll then be able to go back to your seven-day and 365-day plans and start to tweak things. Don't stress about making this happen all at once; just focus on the act of thinking about these three different time horizons, and as you practice Kaizen and continue to improve on your plan, it'll start to come together beautifully. I promise.

To start to think through the next five years, you'll first answer a set of questions that helps you to reflect and learn from the five-year (similar to the one-year) exercise:

1. What are the things I am grateful for?

2. What are the things I am stressed about?

3. What are my key accomplishments over the past five years?

4. Looking back, what did I say I would accomplish in the past five years? How did this go? Are these goals still relevant?

5. Looking back, what are my strengths and secret powers? You've worked on quite a bit over the past five years: Identify the key skills and capabilities you've developed to a point of mastery.

Again, just as with the Unstoppable Sundays and 365-day exercises, don't overthink it. All that is important is that you articulate your thoughts on paper (or screen), so that they're not just percolating in your head.

Once you've completed these questions, you'll have (again) gotten a great handle on just how far you've come from five years ago. You'll have identified your significant accomplishments, the skills you've developed, and what you love spending time on versus what you'd like to do less of. Most importantly, you'll hopefully start to realize just how much you can accomplish over the course of a five-year span.

As the final step, you'll sit down and write out in story form (or letter form) a vision of yourself as you will be five years from now. I want you to sit and close your eyes. You today are grabbing coffee with a stranger. This stranger was introduced to you as a potential mentor who is wildly successful. A mutual friend thought the two of you should meet because you have similar values, goals, and aspirations, and she is much farther ahead and can help you.

So as you're grabbing coffee, the stranger starts to tell you her story. How does she spend her time? What does she do? What excites her? What are the goals that she is working toward? How does she look physically?

This stranger is actually you, five years from now -- after having practiced nearly half a decade of **Belief x Discipline.** After nearly half a decade of Unstoppable Sundays, of planning out her years, and taking focused action in accomplishing her goals.

Write down the story of this person. Go into as much detail as possible and don't hold back. Don't let yourself be limited by what is possible versus what is not (because, remember, we tend to underestimate what we can accomplish in five to ten years). And keep writing until you feel an overwhelming emotion. That's when you'll know you've hit your true north about who you want to become.

As you round out your five-year vision for yourself, here are a few additional questions to ask yourself:

1. Does this feel true? Is there a part of this that Teenage You aspired to?
2. Zooming back into your one-year plan, and your next seven days, are you doing the things today that get you toward becoming this person?
3. What are the circumstances in your current situation that you'd need to eradicate or change in order to become a better version of yourself and closer to this vision of yourself?
4. What would you change about the priorities you've set for yourself for the next seven days to get closer to this vision? How about the next 365 days?

Use our template to work through this easily: To make it even easier to begin the practice of your five-year vision and strategy, we've created a simple template that you can use to get started quickly. You can download it here: https://www.getunstoppable.com/templates/five-year-vision

Much in the spirit of being proactive, you'll use this five-year North Star to guide your decisions going forward. How will you spend your next seven days differently? How about your next 365 days? If you continue to pause and reflect on your next seven days, tweak your plan for your next 365 days, and then enrich your vision for yourself over the next 1,825 days (five years), you can not only start to develop a personal strategy for your life, but you'll also be able to stay tethered to it and to improve it over time. Most importantly, you'll stop being a DABBLER and you'll become a DO-er.

Now remember what we said about this book! This book is not meant to be a piece of art that sits on your bookshelf or one that just gets forgotten.

So grab a pen, and let's work through what you've processed through this chapter.

Chapter 8,
Questions to Ask Yourself

What was the last emergency that came up in your life where you had to completely reorder your schedule to tend to the matter at hand?

What did you do to recover from having to take time away for the emergency? How bad did it get? Were you able to get back on track and on schedule?

Creating a vision for ourselves and a plan for our lives never makes it to the top of our priority lists. And yet doing so can have such a profound impact on our lives, on our ability to provide for ourselves and our loved ones and our family.

What would happen if you treated creating this life plan for yourself like an emergency? What activities could you pause briefly to tend to this matter at hand?

Chapter 8,
Actions to Take

☐ Identify time on your calendar where you can take a half-day: perhaps it is time gained by skipping a party, or not watching a movie, or even by playing hooky from work... So that you can take some time, create some space, and tend to this urgent matter of creating a five-year vision for your life.

☐ Download our Five-year Life Plan template, set it up, and start to commit to creating a proactive five-year vision for yourself: https://www.getunstoppable.com/templates/five-year-vision

☐ Onwards!

Chapter 8,
Bonus Materials

- Watch my episode on Visualize You 5 Years from Now, https://www.getunstoppable.com/your-five-year-self/
- Watch my episode on Jobs and Career in your 20s and 30s, https://www.getunstoppable.com/career
- Watch my episode on 3 Ways to Invest in Yourself, https://www.getunstoppable.com/3-ways-to-invest-in-yourself/

CHAPTER 9:

GET PROACTIVE ABOUT THE FIVE PEOPLE YOU SPEND THE MOST TIME WITH

"You are the average of the five people you spend the most time with."

— Jim Rohn

In this final step, as you're hopefully deep into doing Unstoppable Sundays and executing on your life goals, I want to talk to you about your community of friends and family.

Who are the five people you spend the most time with? Are they as growth-minded as you? Are they taking a proactive approach to life? Truth is, unless you support yourself with other growth-minded people, you will not grow. The inertia is just too much.

In an earlier chapter, I mentioned that there are TWO key reasons why people can't switch from being DABBLERS to DO-ers. There are TWO key reasons why people can't switch from hoping and dreaming to actually achieving. These are the same TWO key reasons that account for the BEFORE in my life and the AFTER in my life:

1. The Dabblers don't have the right actionable framework to go make change happen.

2. The Dabblers don't have the people in their lives who push or inspire them to do it.

You need people around you who are constantly pushing you to do more and be more. I'm not talking about hiring an accountability coach, nor do I mean a best friend or partner who nags at you all day. I'm talking about people who are already performing at the level that you want to be at. They're the ones who are already living the life you want to be living -- and just simply won't hang out with you unless you step up -- because otherwise you'd just be slowing them down.

I'm not saying that this means you need to get rid of your best friends and family. I'm not. However, what I am saying is that if you want to be performing at a different level, you need to start spending more time with the people who are already performing at that level.

Which is why, as the final step of the book, I'm extending you a personal invitation to join our Unstoppable Life Program & Community: https://getunstoppable.com/life

There's a reason why I bring this up only at the end. It's for people who are truly committed to becoming the best version of themselves and who are starting out on that journey – just like you.

In order for you to succeed in becoming Unstoppable, you must take stock of the people in your life and start to level up.

Now remember what we said about this book! This book is not meant to be a piece of art that sits on your bookshelf or one that just gets forgotten. So grab a pen, and let's work through what we've talked about in this chapter.

Chapter 9,
Questions to Ask Yourself

Who are the five people you spend the most of your work and leisure time with? A good trick to figuring this out is looking at your phone and seeing the five people you text the most often.

If you were to print out your wildest goals over the next five years and show it to each of them, how would they react? Would they laugh? Would they be skeptical? Would they think you're crazy? Who in the group would say, "Yeah... Let me show you my goals..."

99

If you were to look beyond your big five, and think about everyone you know, who is pushing him or herself and going after the same type of goals as you? Who is the person who is chasing down their dreams with the level of energy, belief, and discipline that is needed to actually achieve those goals?

Chapter 9,
Actions to Take

☐ Who are the people in your life who are holding you back from achieving your goals?

☐ Who are the people in your life who inspire you and are pushing as hard as you should be pushing to achieve the life they want for themselves?

☐ How can you respectfully and with love – spend less time with the people who are holding you back?

☐ How can you spend more time with the people who will propel you forward?

☐ What new communities, conferences, meetups, and/or online groups can you join with more like-minded people?

☐ Join our community and connect with others following the Unstoppable life: https://getunstoppable.com/community

☐ Onwards!

CHAPTER 10:

IN CONCLUSION, AND CONTINUING YOUR JOURNEY TO BECOME UNSTOPPABLE

learned (almost too late) in my life that developing a PROACTIVE approach to my days led to a calmer me. A less frantic me.

I spent a significant part of my youth as a person who constantly wanted to do "what's right." I wanted to please others, especially my elders and my parents. I grew up inclined to think about optics and how things look, and I prioritized things that I thought would bring me happiness -- but that ultimately failed to do so. I became incredibly great at setting and crushing goals, but they consistently turned out to be the wrong goals.

Through my 20s, I constantly did things based on what I thought society expected of me -- or what I thought you were supposed to do. This desire to please others led to me marrying a wonderful person at the young age of 25 -- which led to a divorce. It led me to pursue a job in finance that produced career success, but left me wholly unfulfilled. Ultimately, I discovered that I had created a life that was careening along at 90 mph on curvy roads, but at the end of the day, I found myself asking: Is this it?

Through this experience, I learned that while you can have anything you want, you can't have everything. So you better get proactive and pick what you want.

And so I made a change. I decided to become more proactive about my life. I decided to focus more on what was important to me and on my dreams, and I focused on substance instead of optics. Most importantly, instead of letting others or society as a whole set the agenda for my life, I started to be more proactive about my life. I made the changes necessary to follow a life path that was true to myself, one Unstoppable Sunday at a time.

As I crushed goals, moved the goalpost to bigger challenges, in my late 20s, and as I entered my 30s, I started to come to terms with a few realizations:

- If you set a goal and define a purpose, you can achieve anything that you want.
- You will never be perfect, you'll never nail the goal perfectly, but even allowing for the speed bumps along the way, with resilience you can accomplish anything and be Unstoppable.
- Not everyone will believe in you in the beginning, but you will never have to explain your success in the end; they'll come around.
- No matter your circumstances, socioeconomic status, level of wealth... Ultimately knowledge is power and with enough knowledge and grit you can accomplish anything. Fortunately for us, knowledge is widely accessible today.
- Given the above, you can indeed be Unstoppable in life, but you have to pay careful attention to what it is you choose to be Unstoppable in.

Through my 20s and 30s, I've worked at the world's largest hedge fund; I started a company from scratch and built it into a multi-million-dollar business while partnering with one of the world's best venture capital firms; and I then sold that company (twice over) while working with the world's best enterprise software private equity firm. I finally started to unlock levels of success that felt right and true to my own path -- all because I decided to become more proactive about life.

During this journey, and through my trials and tribulations, I picked up a specific set of skills and insights into what it takes to pick the right goals in your life, go after them, and win. I learned that it's not enough to know how to crush goals; it's equally important to pick the right goals -- those that are true to yourself and your purpose on this planet. Most importantly, I learned that with anything worthwhile, there will always be bumps in the road, and that those who can build resilience and persevere will become Unstoppable in this life.

All of this wraps around the simple idea of being more PROACTIVE in your life through Belief and Discipline. Shockingly, none of this knowledge needed to be learned from experience. None of this knowledge is taught at schools. And yet it was plainly available in age-old books that were readily available -- sadly, it isn't in plain sight to the average person.

Unstoppable is the movement I created to share everything that I've learned. It's the idea that with **Belief x Discipline**, you can be more proactive in life and achieve your wildest dreams. It's the idea that if we can take this common knowledge around designing and living a more proactive life, and if we persuade even 1,000 people to be ten percent more proactive, we will forever tilt the axis of the planet.

This life planning book is our first real educational system covering some of our most basic principles on how to design and live a proactive life -- and we expect to do more. Thank you for being part of our movement, and I hope the core ideas we present in this book help you go on to practice Belief and Discipline every day, and go on to do incredible things for our planet.

If there is one core concept I want you to walk away with from this book, it is this: You can either let life happen to you, or you can take control of your life. Somewhere in the middle of that is a beautiful equilibrium where universal forces collude with your innermost desires to help you manifest the beautiful life you deserve. This equilibrium point is the perfect balance of being proactive and refusing what is not right for you, while opening up to what the universe is guiding you to.

In the beginning of this book, I made a simple promise to you: I'd teach you the tools I utilize regularly to live a more proactive life. These tools and processes unlocked over a decade of productivity and success for me, my career, and my family:

- **In Chapter 5,** I introduced you to the idea of practicing Unstoppable Sundays, where we taught you to reflect on and plan for your next seven days.
- **In Chapter 6,** I helped you zoom out and start to think about your one-year plan by answering a set of very pointed questions that help you practice gratitude, assess where you are today, and then start to lay out a plan for the next 365 days.
- **In Chapter 7,** I introduced a new tool that you can use to become proactive about the 365 days you're given every year, so that you can be proactive about how you spend your days and months in a given year, and make tough trade-offs on what you spend your time on versus not.
- **In Chapter 8,** I helped you really zoom out, take a long-term unconstrained view, and think about the next five years of your life and the vision you want to set for yourself.
- **In Chapter 9,** I walked you through the most significant impediment in your life relative to achieving your goals (the five people you spend the most time with).

Through every exercise, through every chapter, I stressed one thing: It doesn't have to be perfect.

The majority of the people on planet Earth do not bother to sit down to pause and reflect, and even fewer set goals and check in on them on a regular basis.

Even by starting to do this and by developing the discipline of practicing Kaizen on your personal life strategy, even by tethering yourself to a strategy and plan -- you're putting yourself into the top of the planet's population.

So, it doesn't have to be perfect. What you DO have to do is the following:

1. Stop DABBLING and switch to becoming a DO-er.
2. Keep practicing Unstoppable Sundays and pause and reflect on your next seven days.
3. Check in on your 365-day goals every month and course-correct as necessary.
4. Keep honing in on your five-year vision for yourself and navigate toward that North Star.

I kept rinsing and repeating on these four key steps over and over and over for nearly a decade and accomplished and achieved the life that I always wanted. I want you to live that way, too.

Chapter 10,
Actions to Take

☐ Kick off another 45-day challenge to dramatically move forward a specific 365-day goal you've set for yourself.

☐ Your journey doesn't have to be lonely. The Unstoppable Community is here to grow with you. Unstoppable, today, is a movement spanning the globe, with tens of thousands of people. You can join our community here: https://getunstoppable.com/life.

Belief x Discipline makes you Unstoppable

·

We're at the end, Dear Reader. I'm so incredibly excited for you. Here's what you can do next.

SHARE THIS BOOK

Please write a review on Amazon and tell others who you think will enjoy this book. Spreading the word helps to reach new readers, grow this movement and the continued production of similar content.

JOIN OUR UNSTOPPABLE LIFE PROGRAM

You can also join our exclusive online Unstoppable Life Program & Web-Based Application for practicing Unstoppable Sunday that helps you dramatically move forward with a specific goal you've set for yourself as part of your life plan. https://getunstoppable.com/life

UNSTOPPABLE SAAS

If you're entrepreneurial or are already running a company, I also invite you to watch my Youtube channel where I apply these principles in becoming a High Performing CEO and Founder to build an Unstoppable strategy for your business. https://getunstoppable.com/youtube

PAY IT FORWARD

I wrote this book because I wanted to pay forward the blessings I received in my life and help others from my experiences. You don't necessarily need to write a book (although I hope that you do someday), but you can also pay it forward today by telling five friends about this book.

About the Author

TK Kader is a business builder, a life and business strategist, and an eternal optimist. He believes that you can achieve anything through belief, discipline and an Unstoppable strategy. TK worked at Bridgewater Associates (one of the best hedge funds in the world). He then founded ToutApp (backed by Andreessen Horowitz and Jackson Square, two of the best venture capital firms in the world). TK sold ToutApp to Marketo (then owned by Vista Equity Partners, one of the best private equity firms in the world) and was part of the executive team at Marketo that helped drive its transformation and eventual $4.75bn sale to Adobe. TK now leads the Unstoppable movement of high performing B2B SaaS CEOs where he helps them build and execute on an Unstoppable Strategy in their life and in their business.

Printed in Great Britain
by Amazon

33240341R00076